The Brain House

Written by: Donesa Walker
Design by: Will Baten

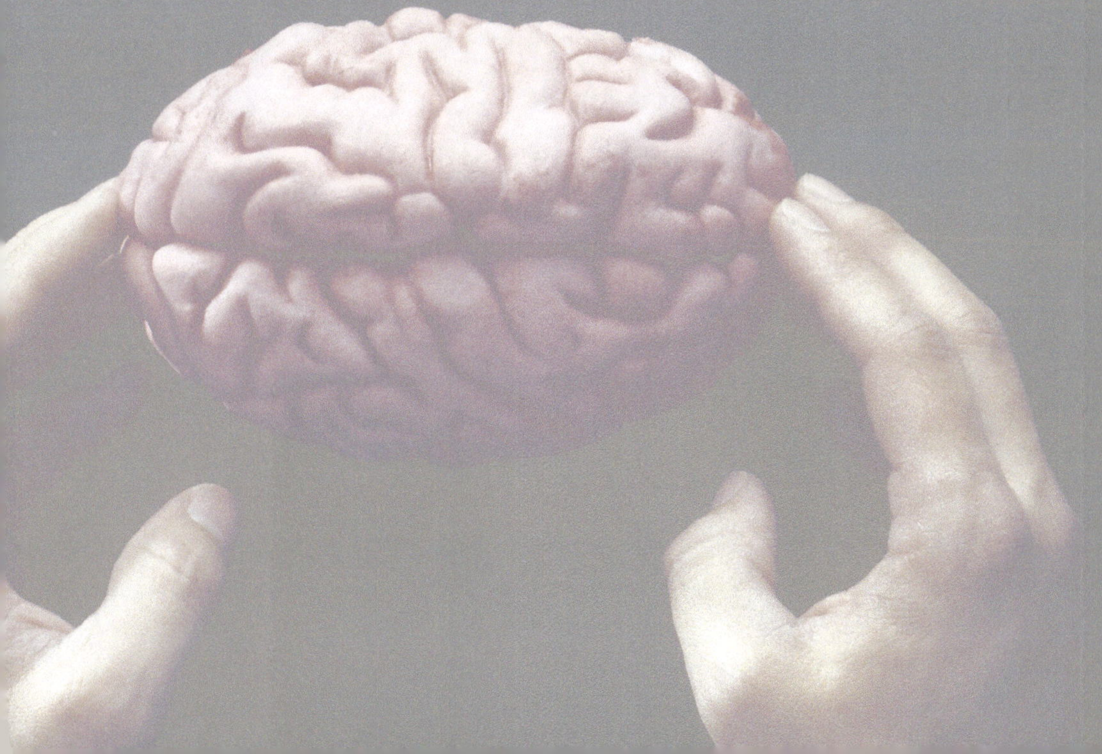

The house I am living
in needs some repair.

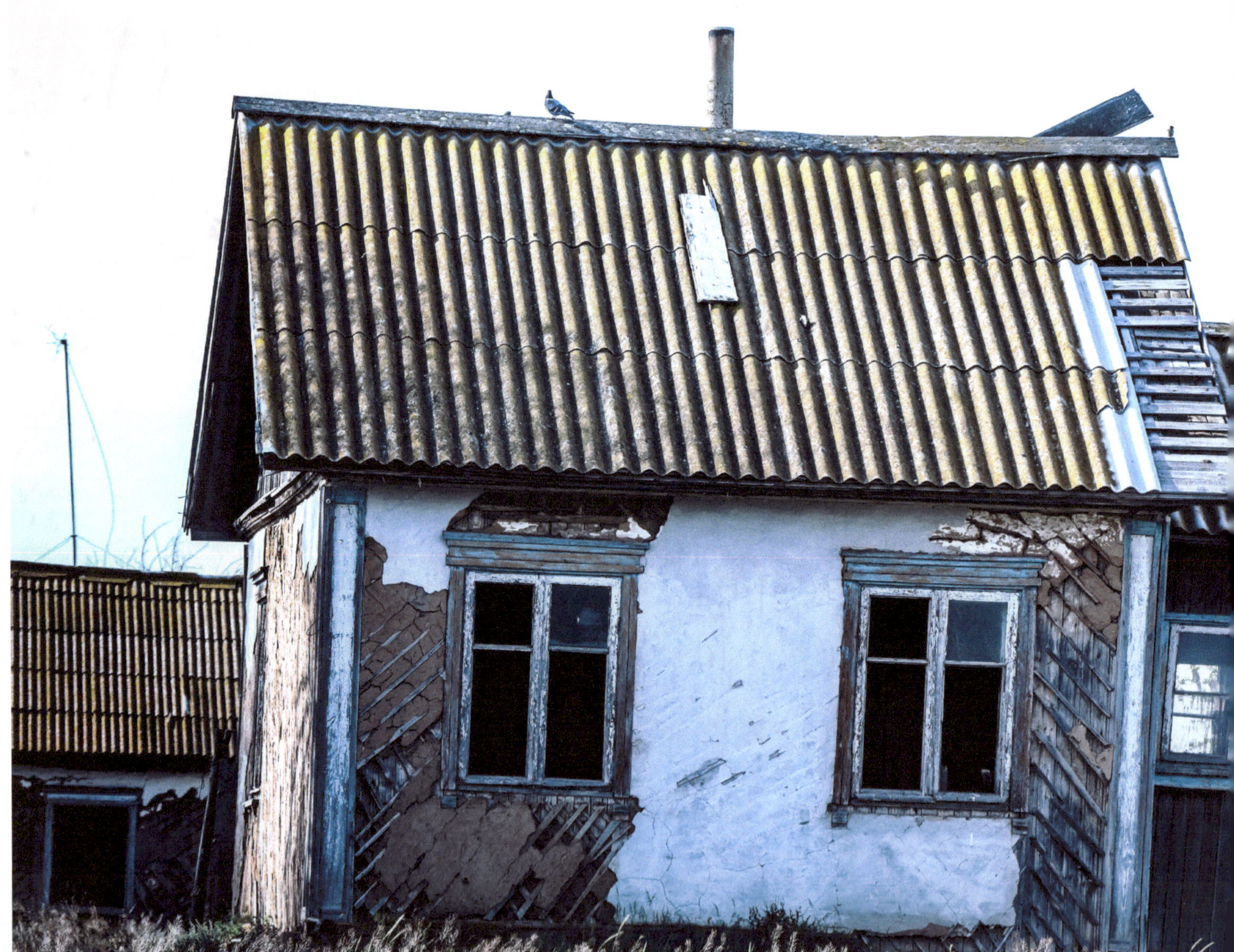

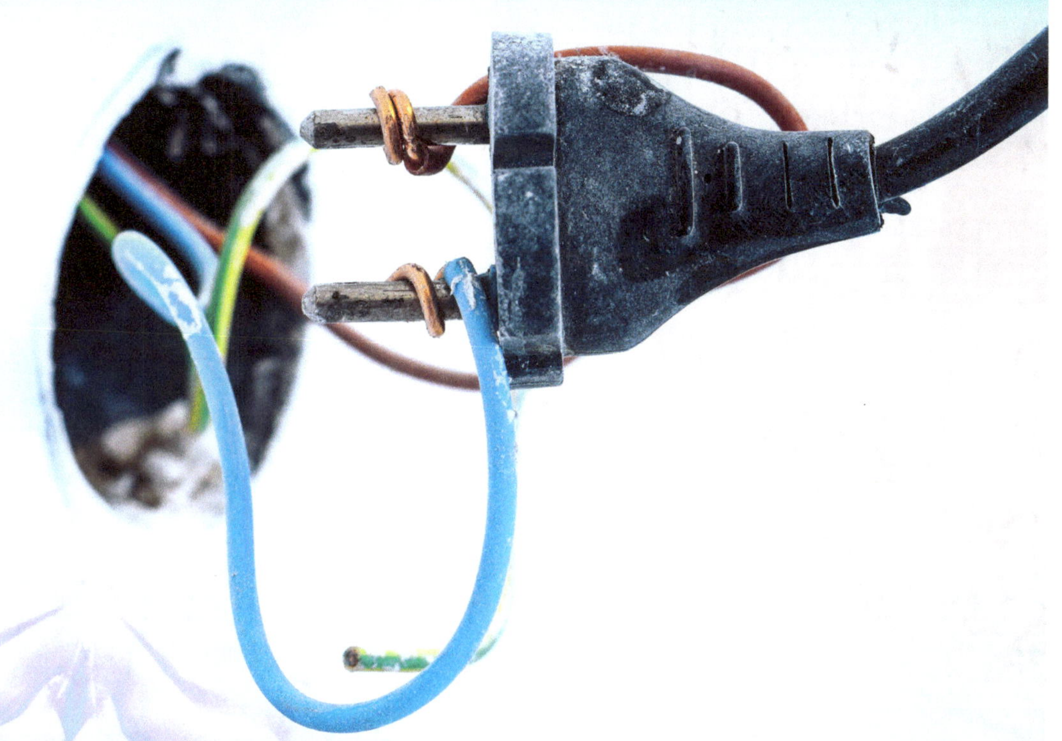
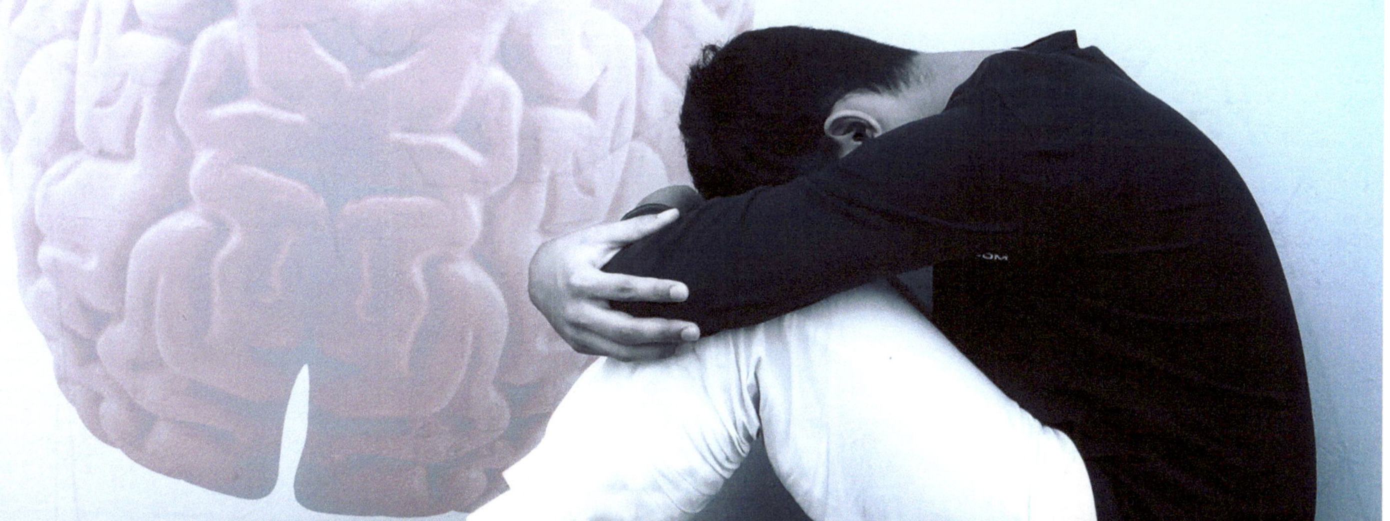

The wiring doesn't
work sometimes.

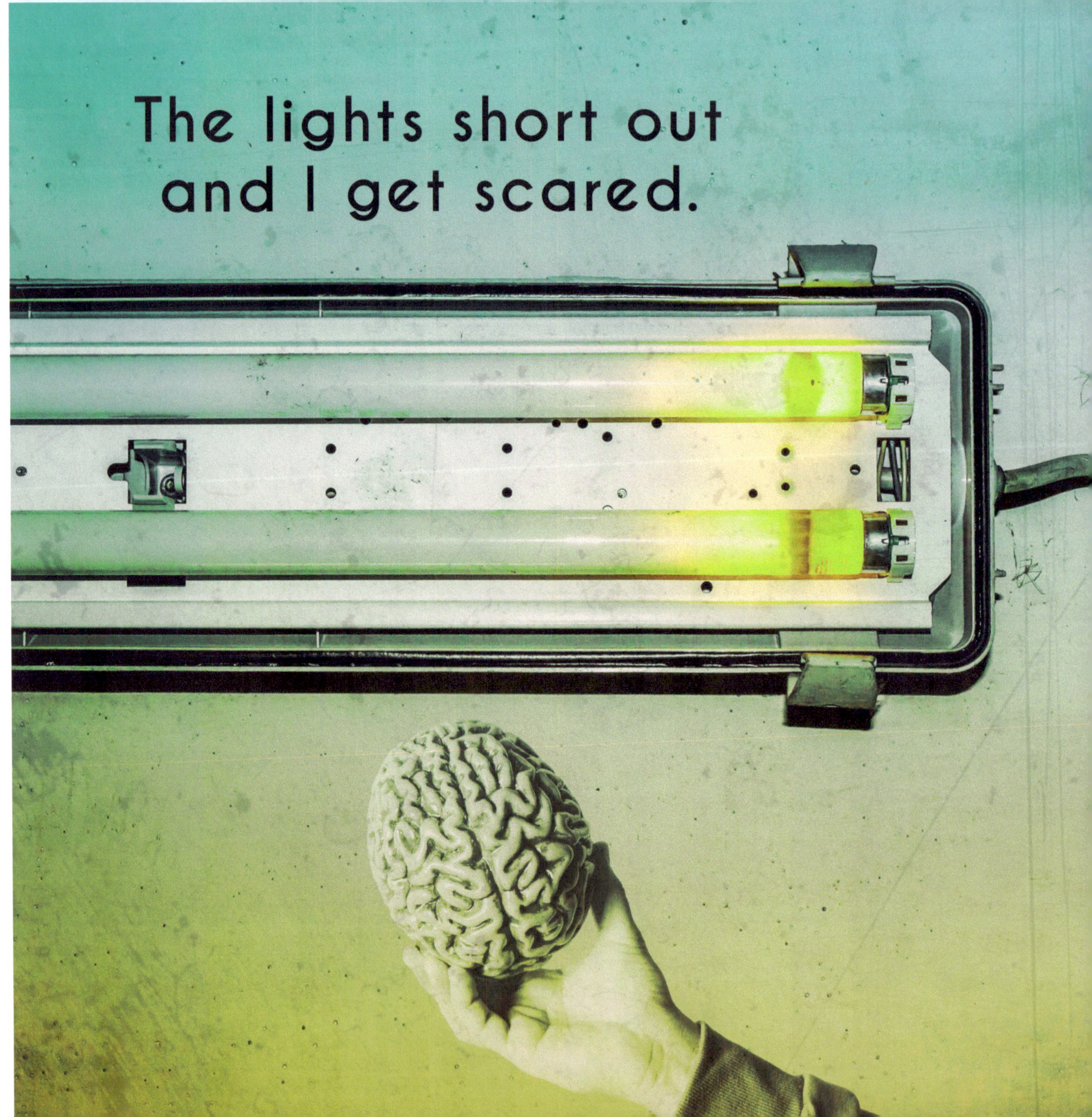
The lights short out
and I get scared.

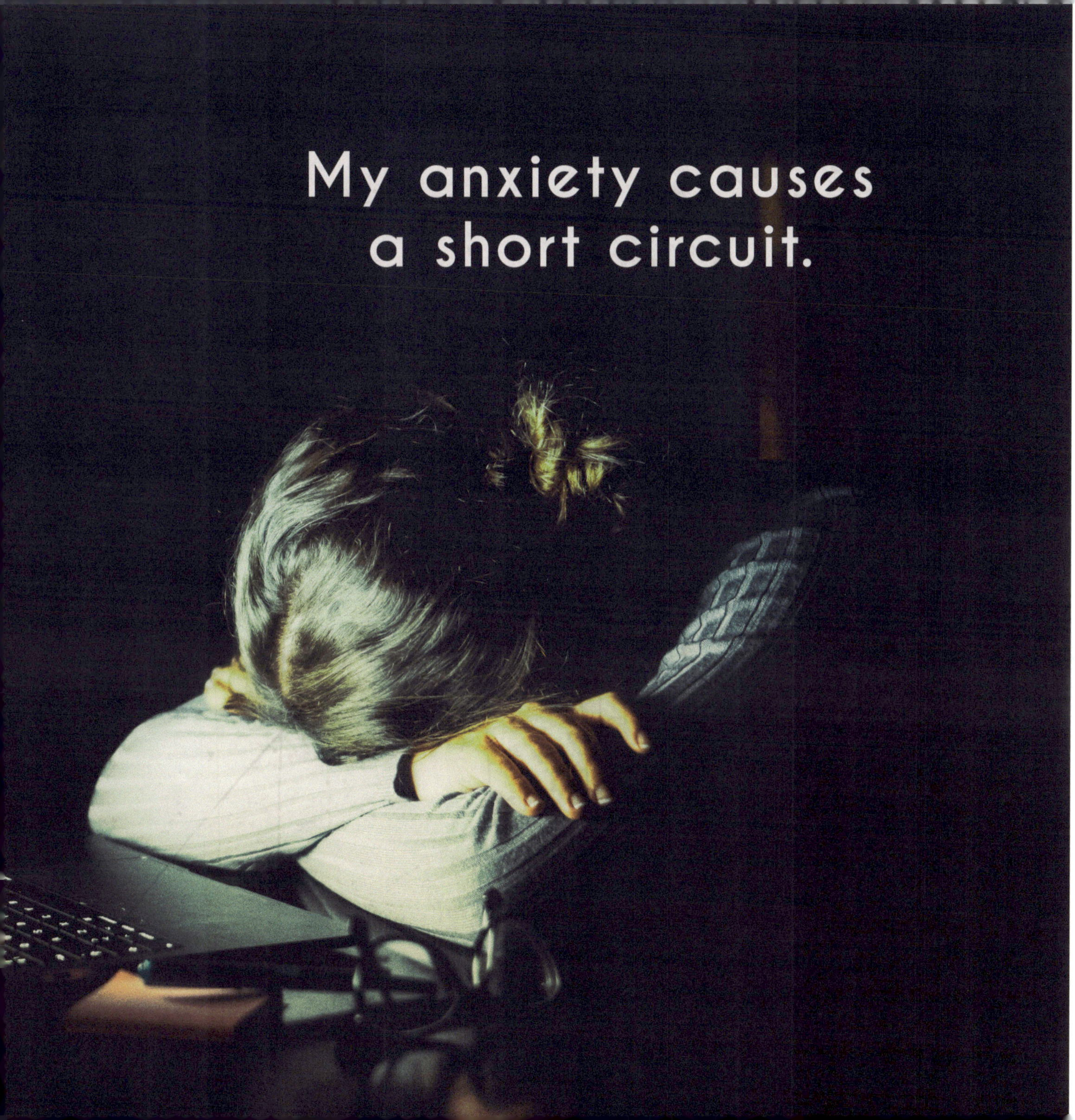

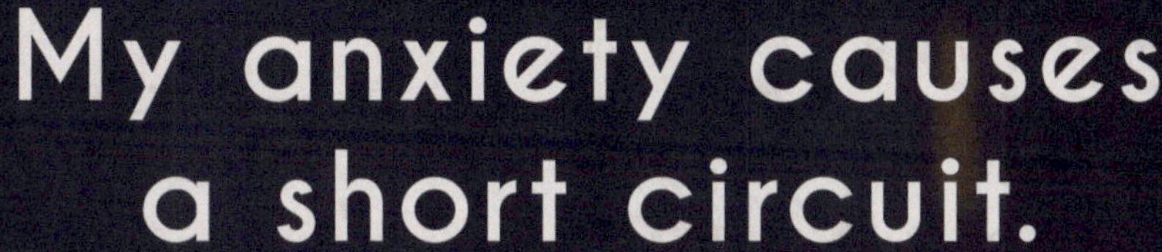
My anxiety causes
a short circuit.

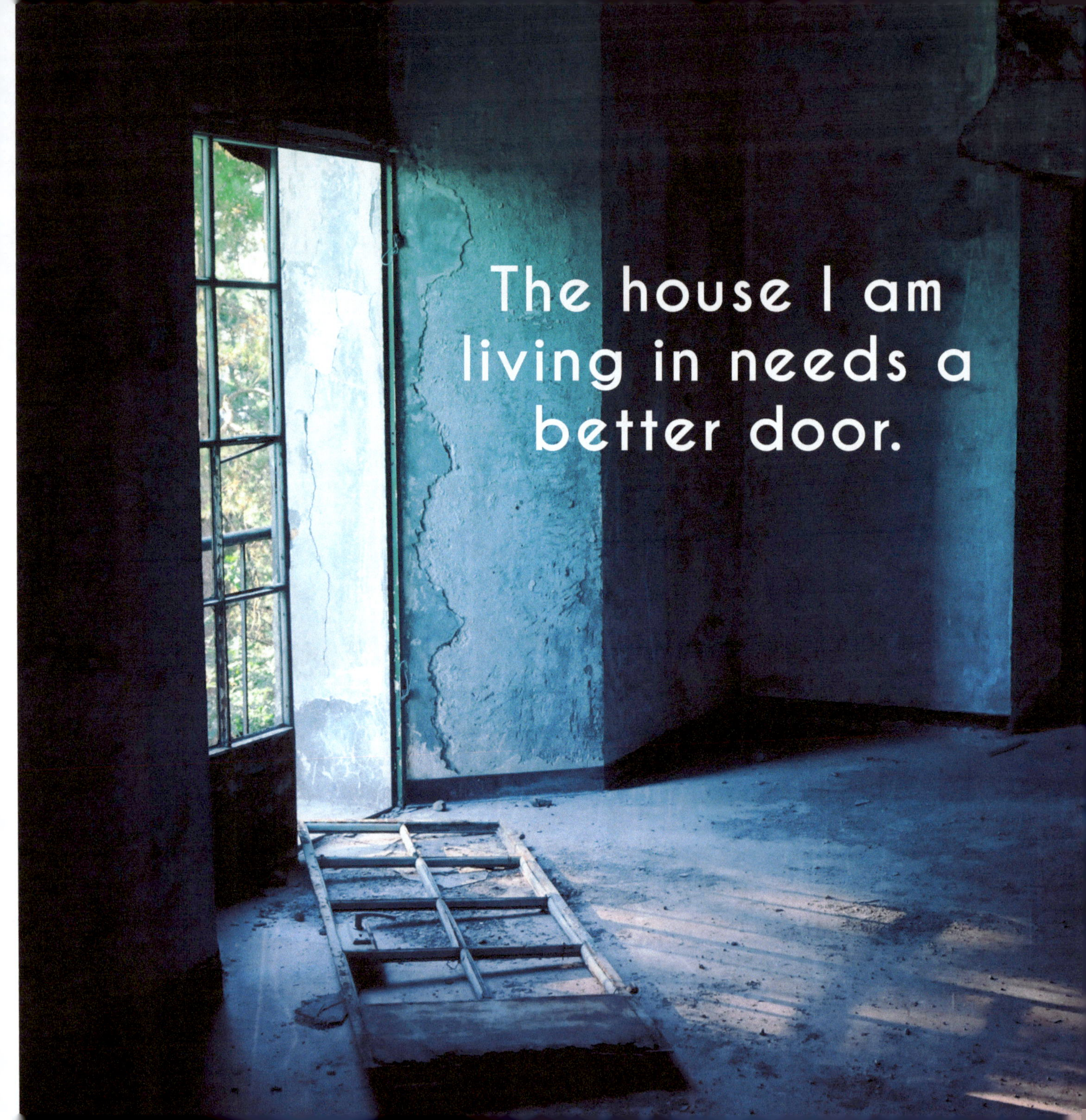
The house I am
living in needs a
better door.

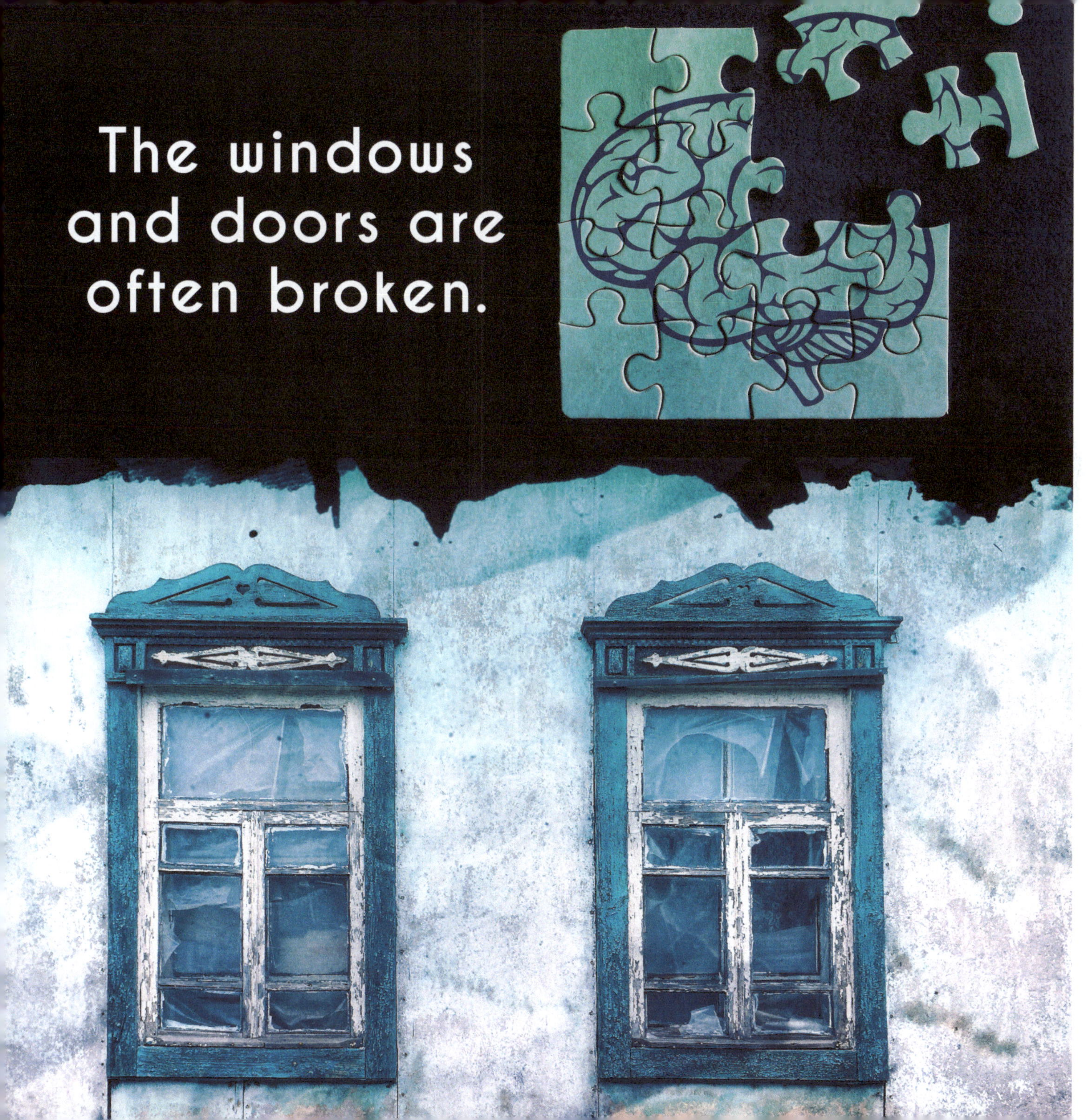
The windows
and doors are
often broken.

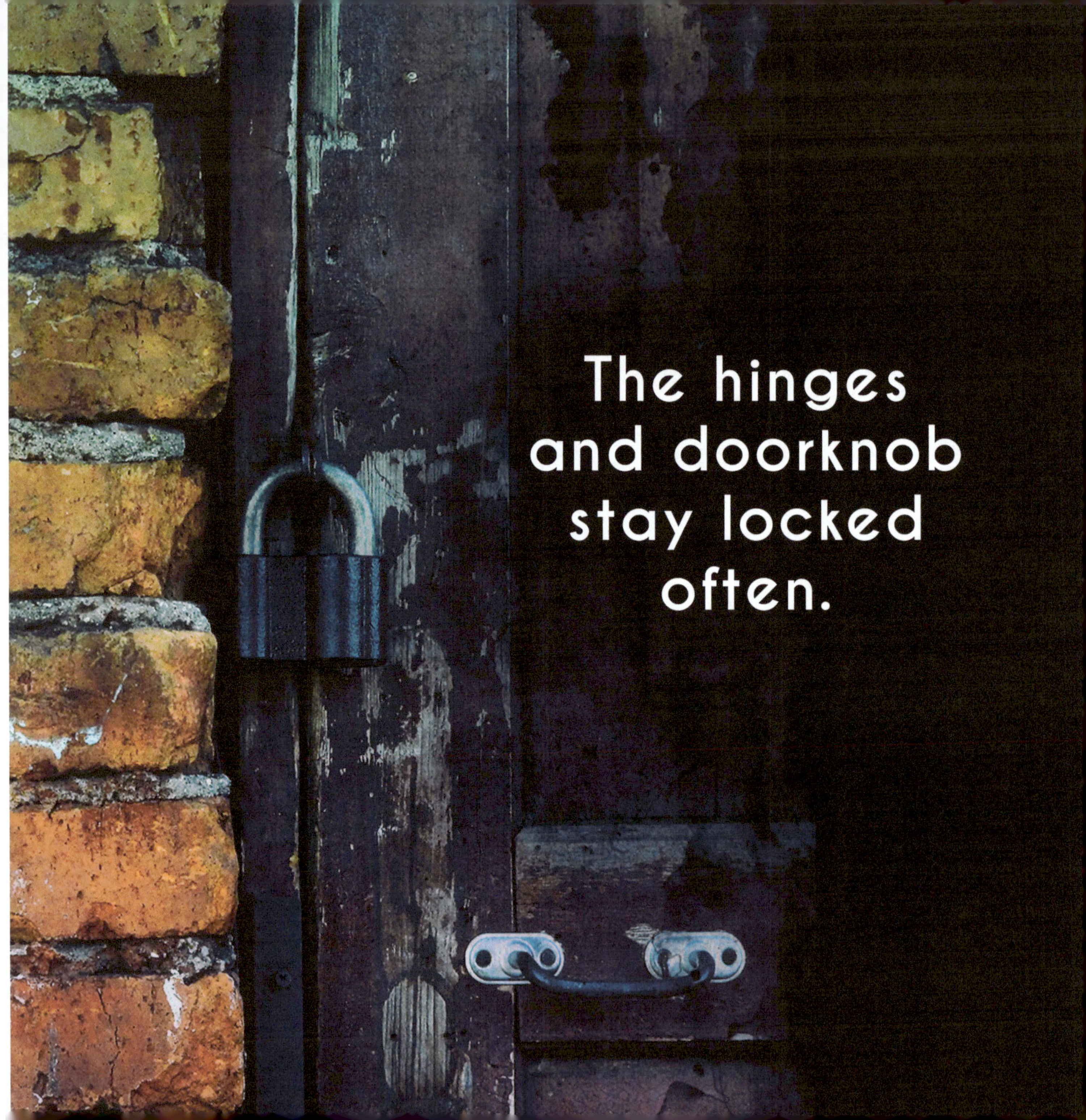
The hinges
and doorknob
stay locked
often.

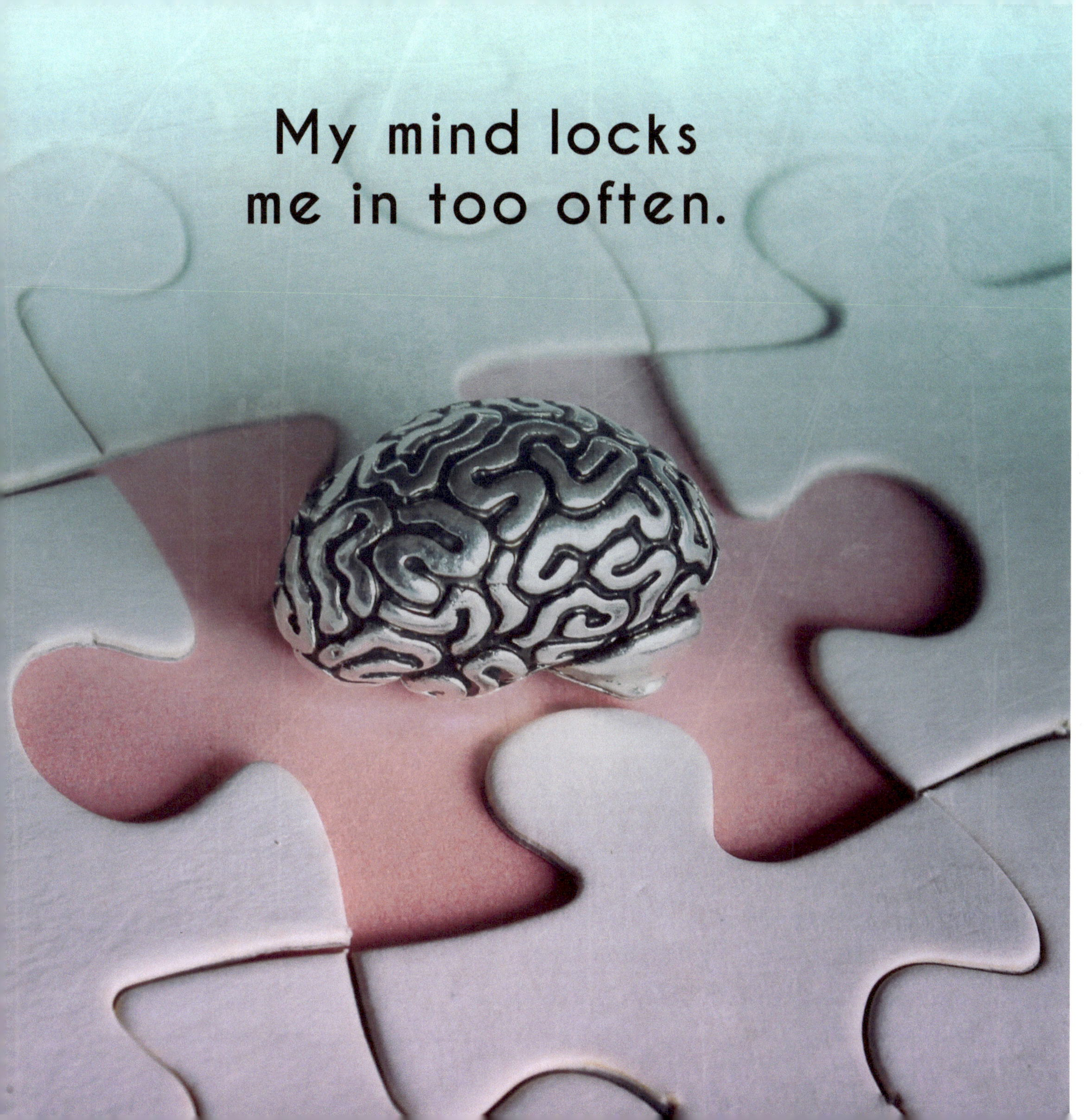
My mind locks
me in too often.

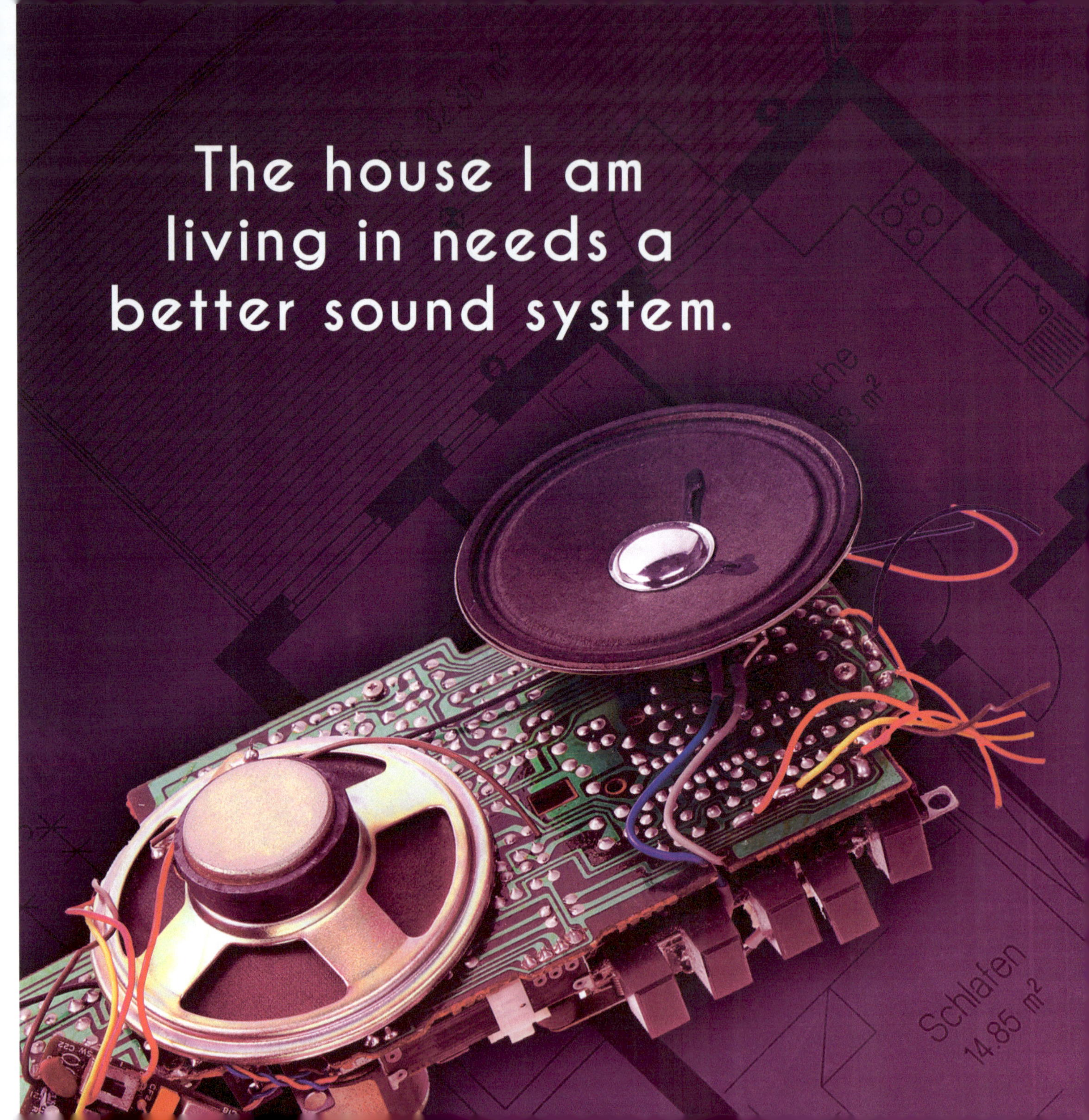

The house I am
living in needs a
better sound system.

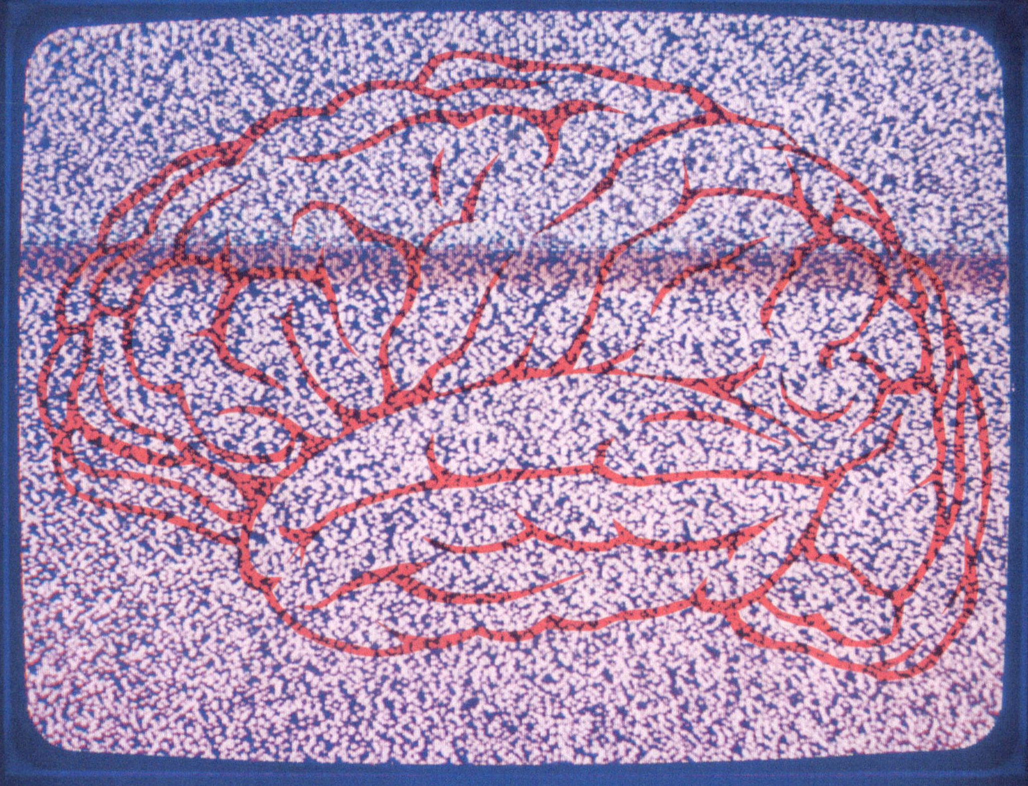

The speakers do not work all the time and the video often gets stuck in slow motion.

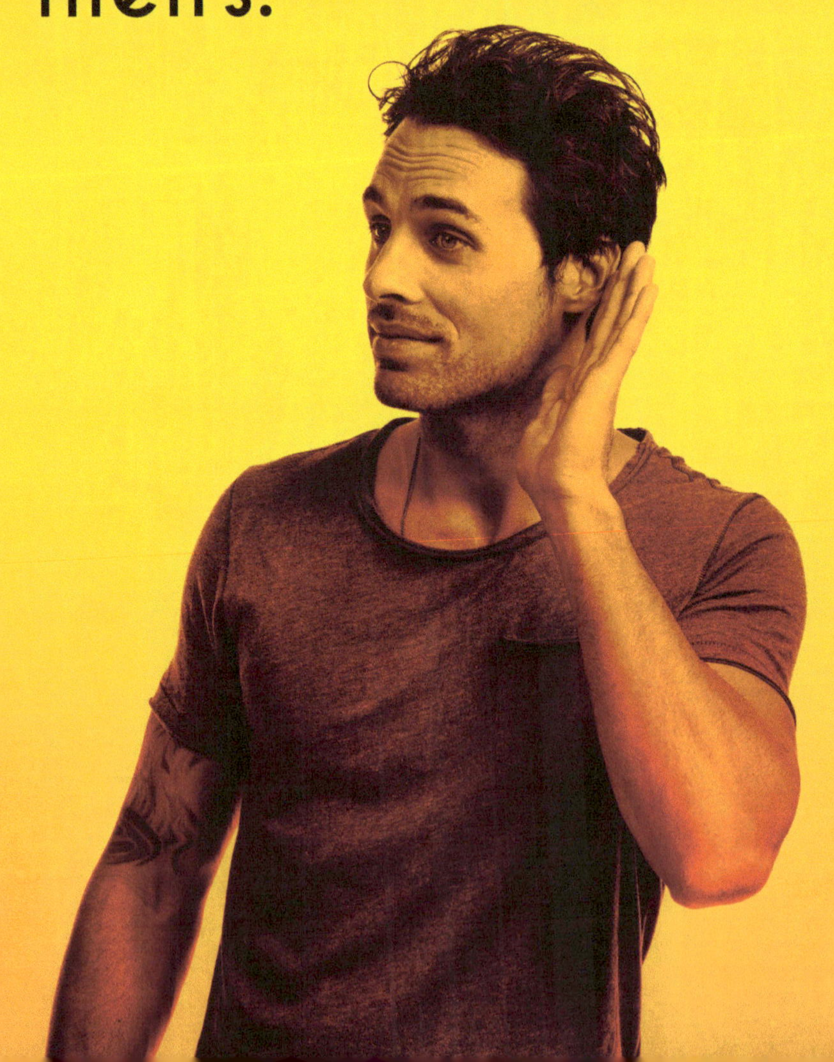
The people cannot
hear my thoughts
and I cannot hear
theirs.

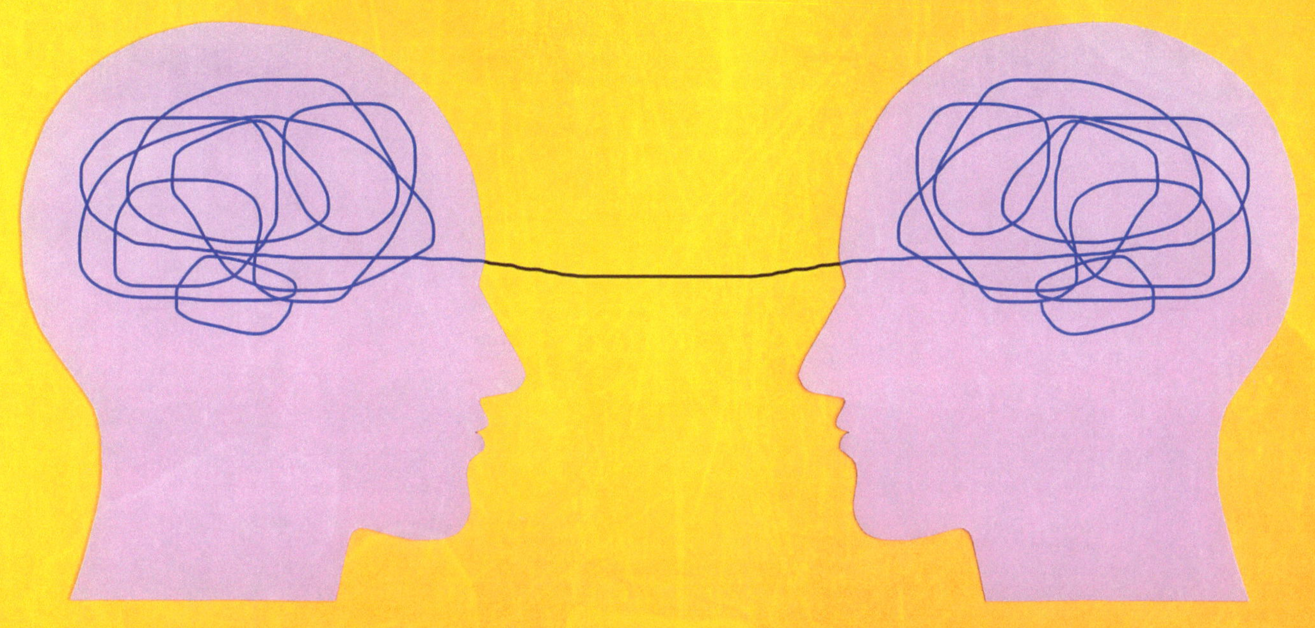

My ears don't process
language very fast.

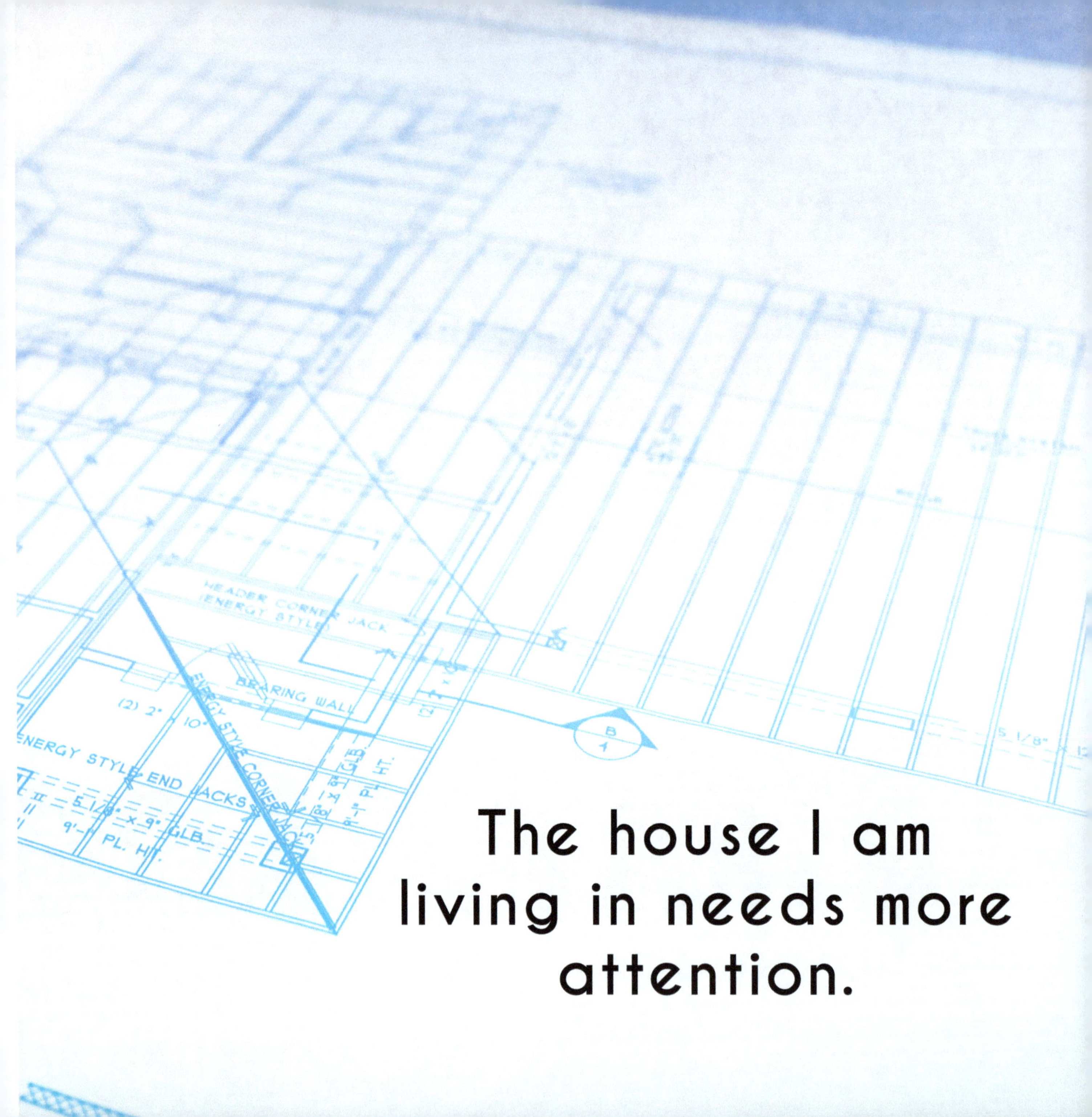

The house I am
living in needs more
attention.

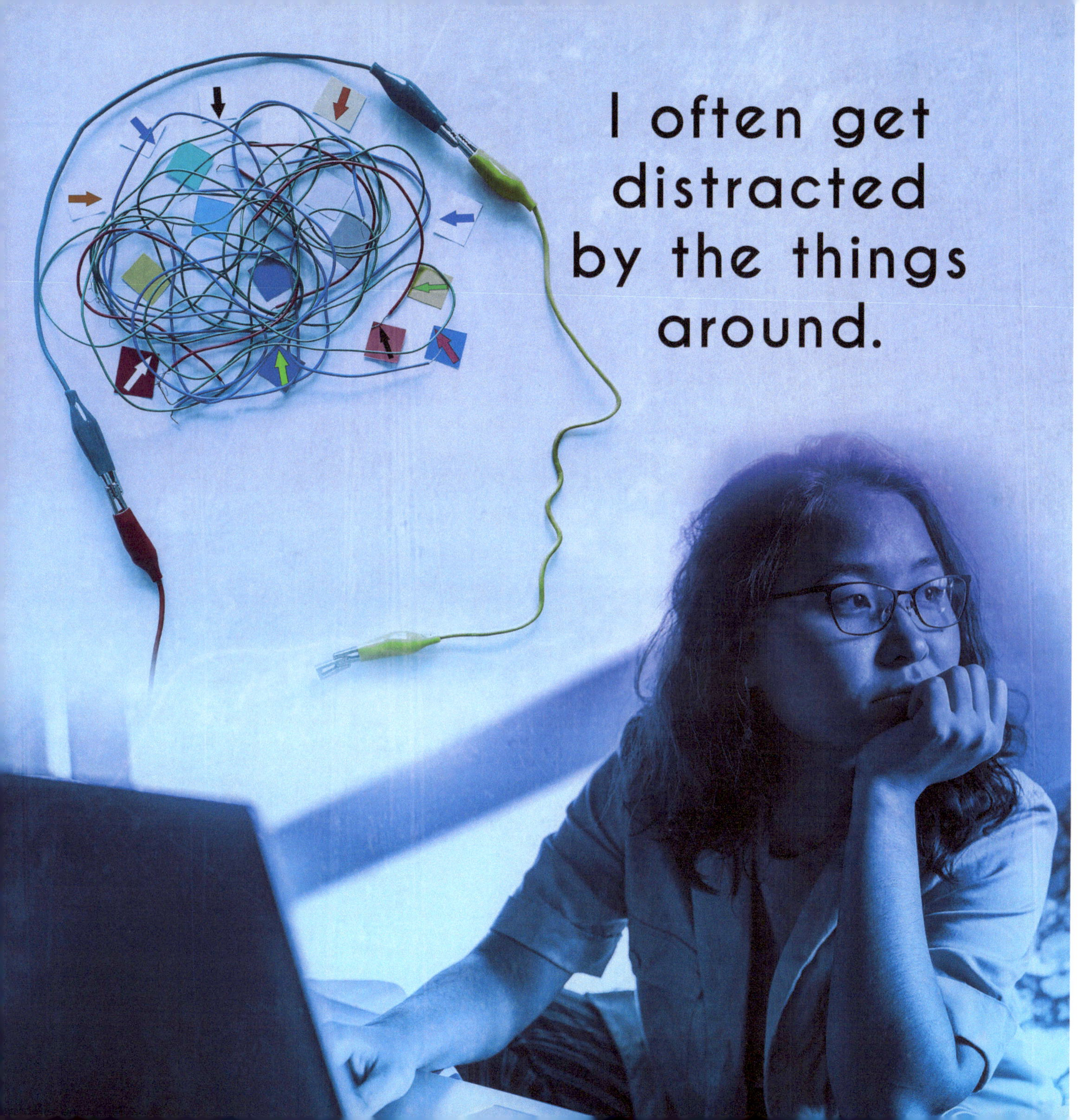
I often get
distracted
by the things
around.

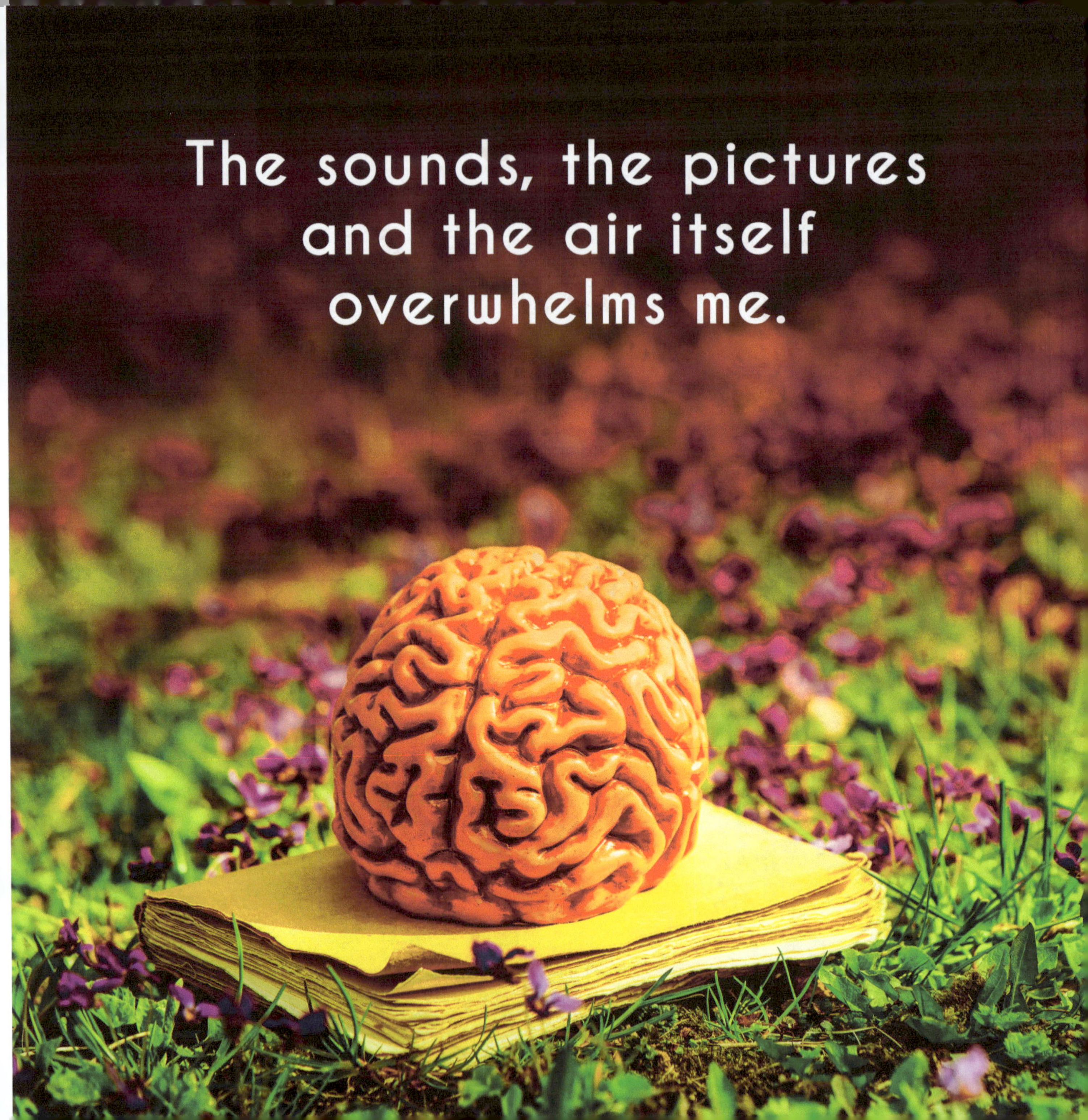
The sounds, the pictures
and the air itself
overwhelms me.

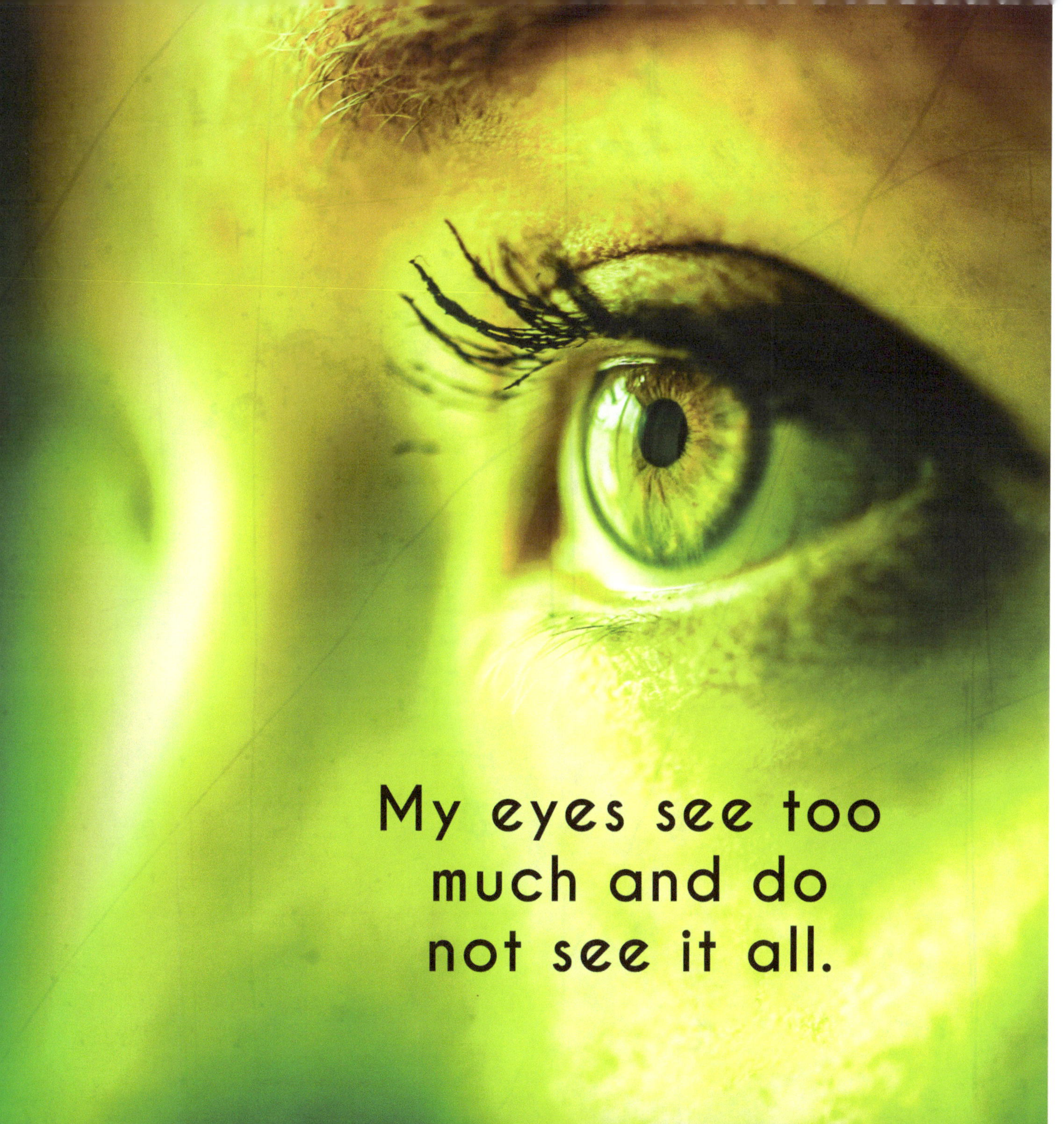
My eyes see too
much and do
not see it all.

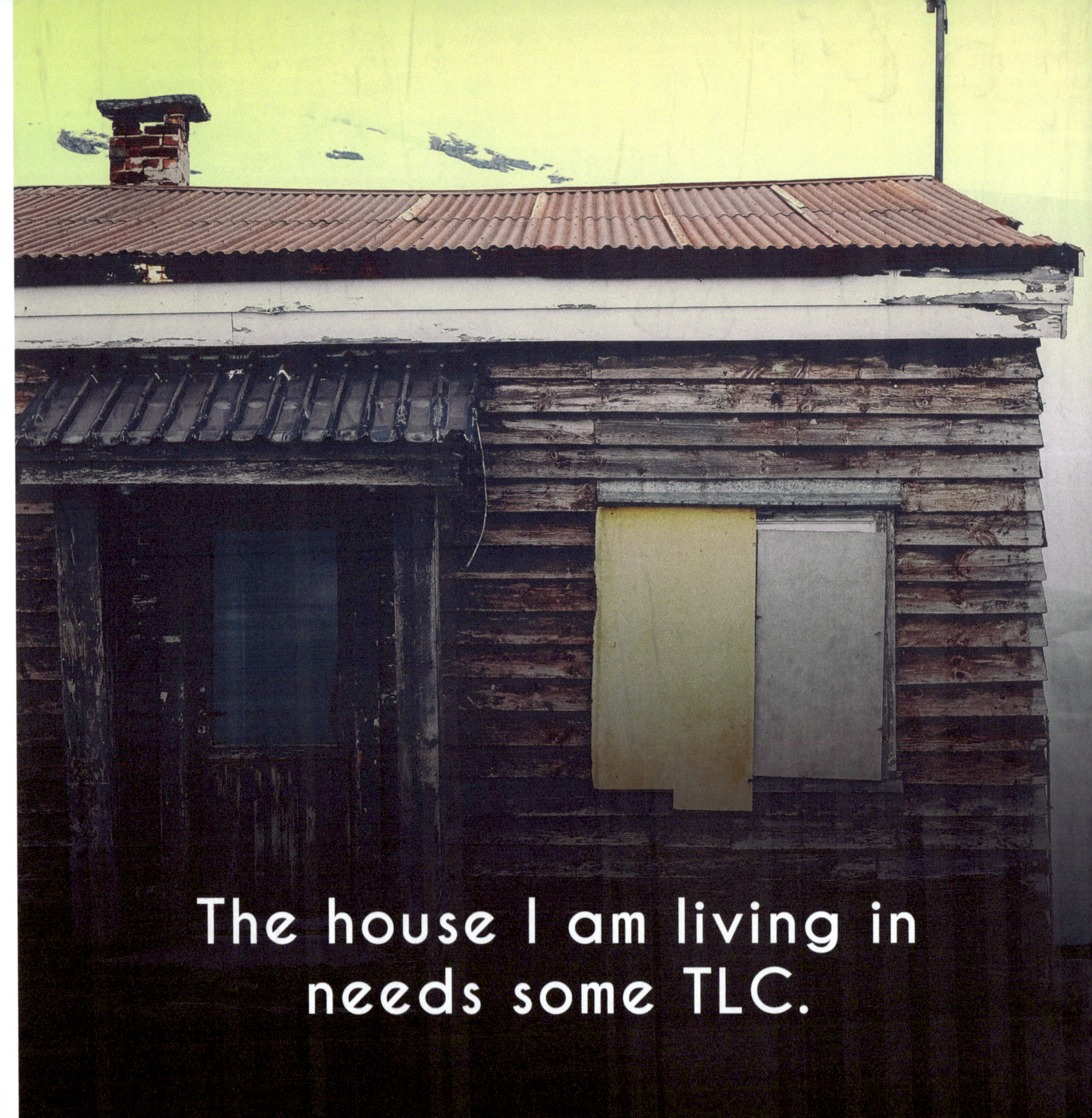
The house I am living in
needs some TLC.

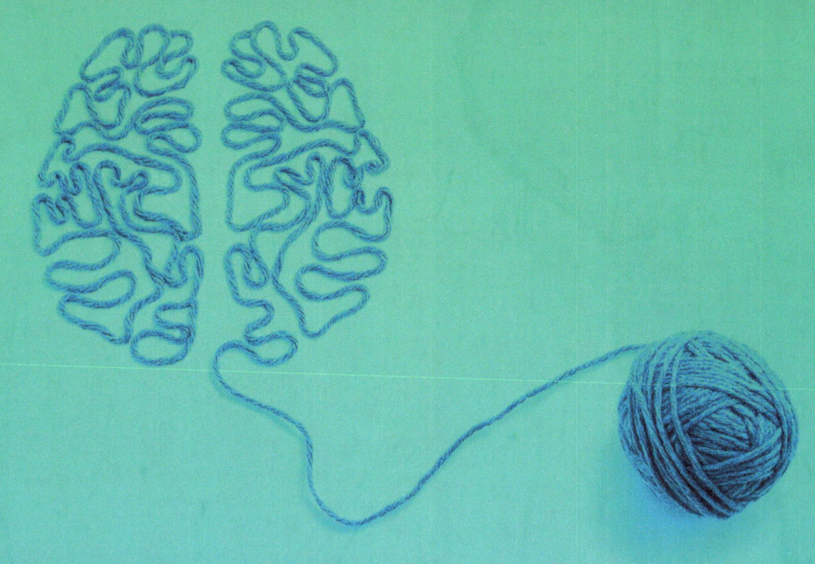

A little paint and new gutters with trim do not seem to change the house inside.

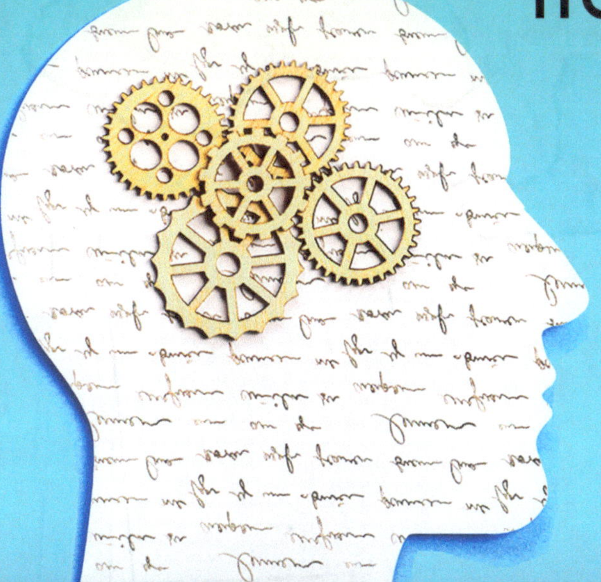

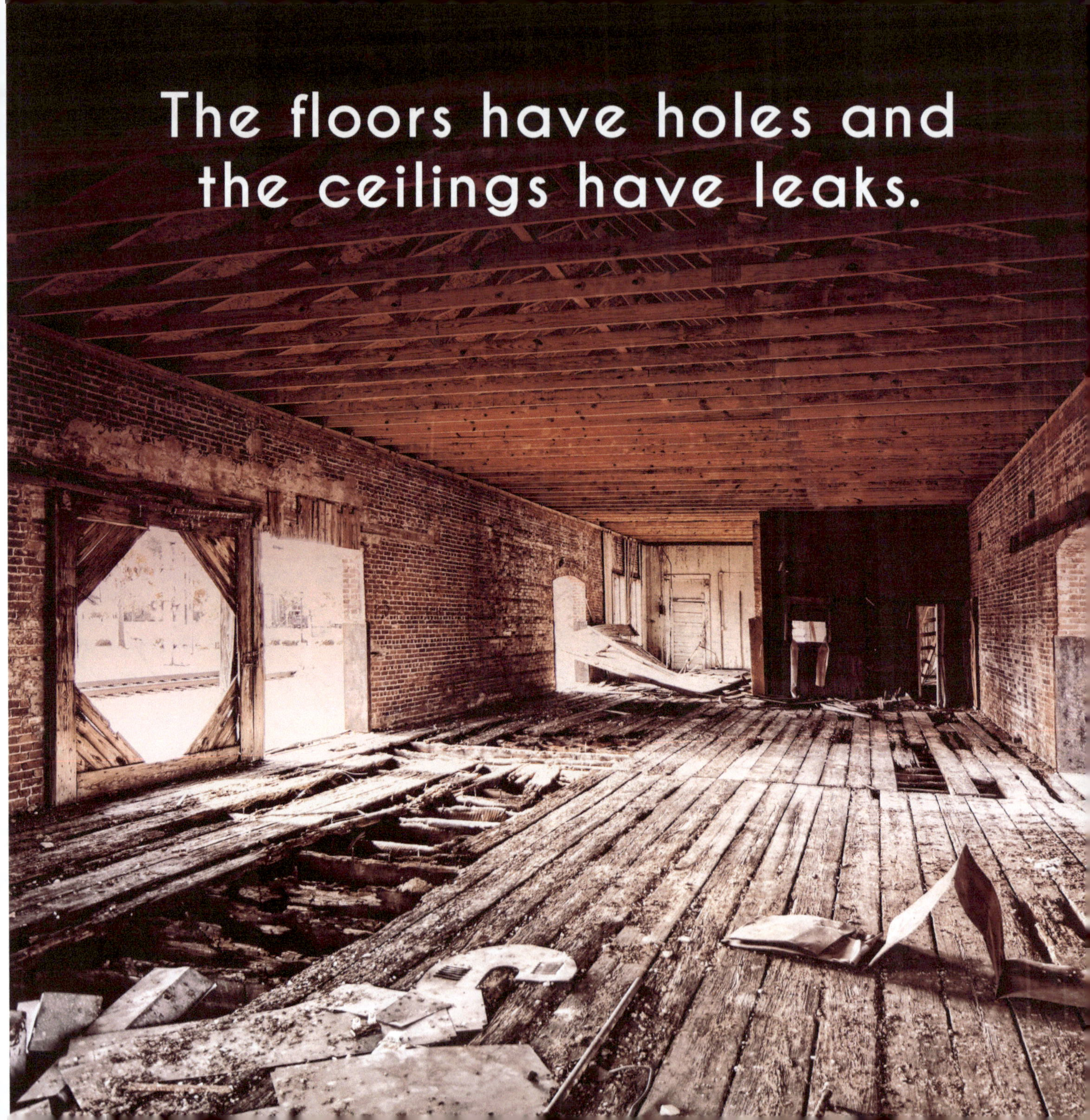

The floors have holes and the ceilings have leaks.

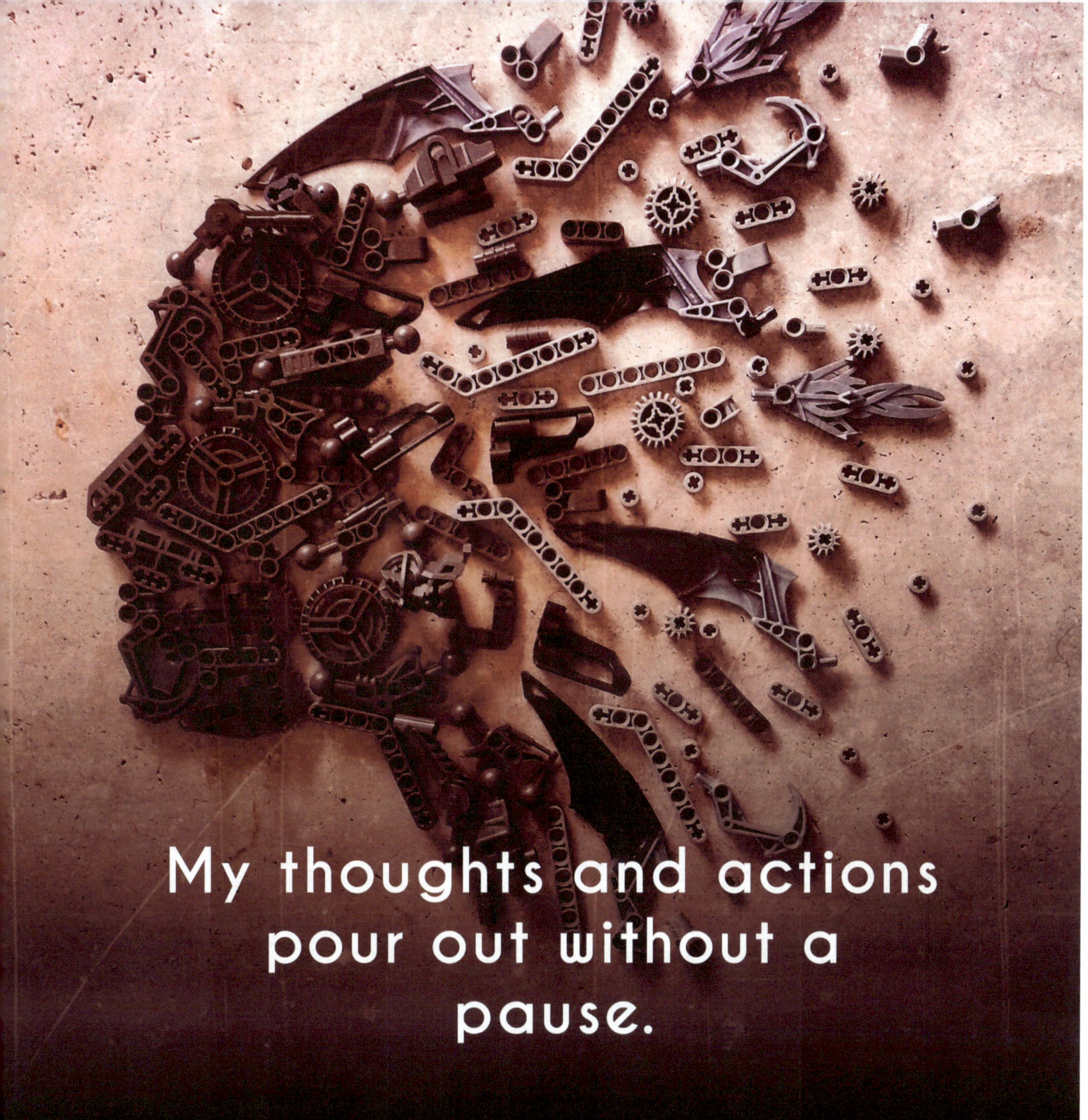

My thoughts and actions
pour out without a
pause.

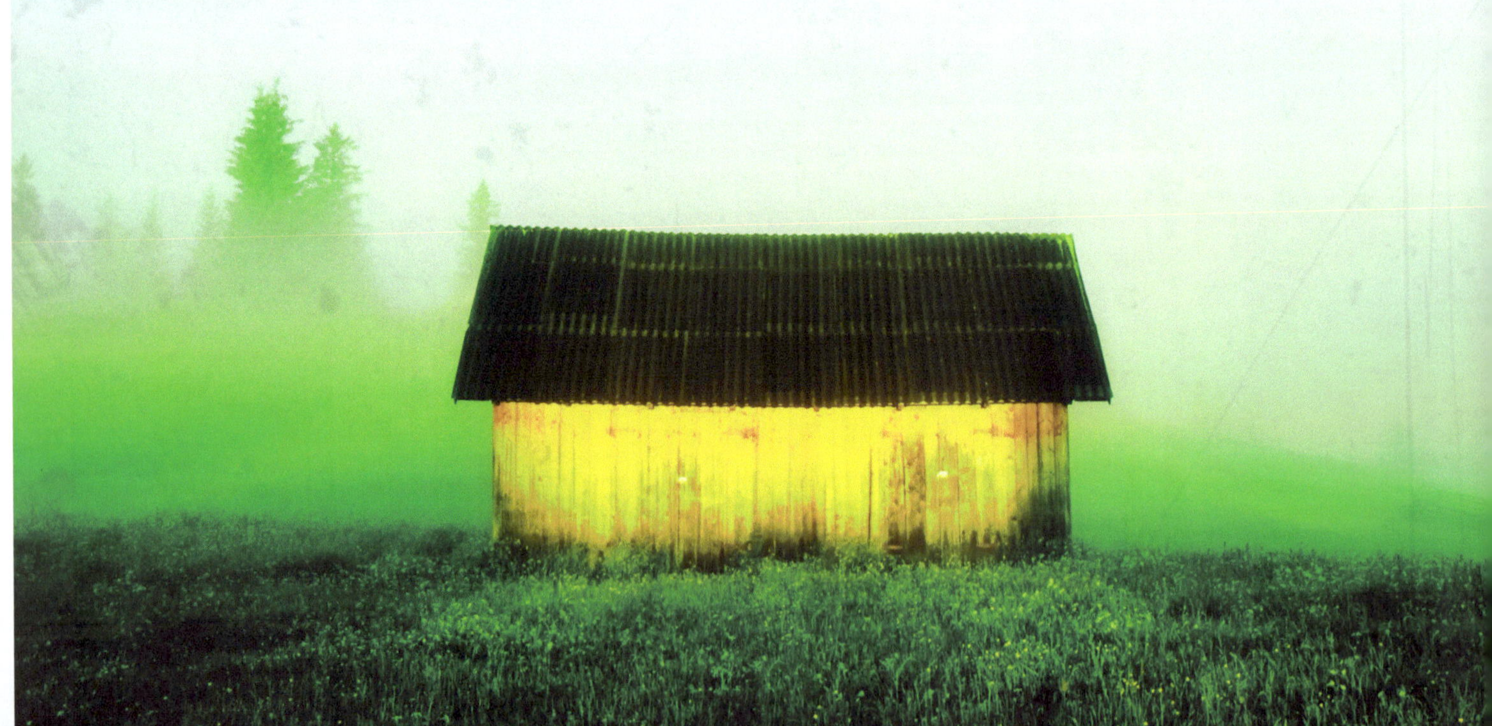
The house I am living in
was given to me.

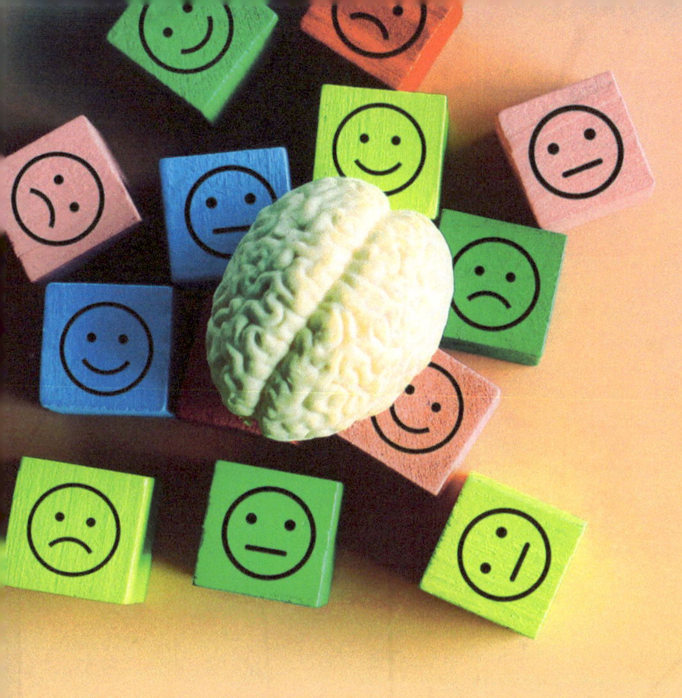

It is the only house I know but some-times I wish I had another house.

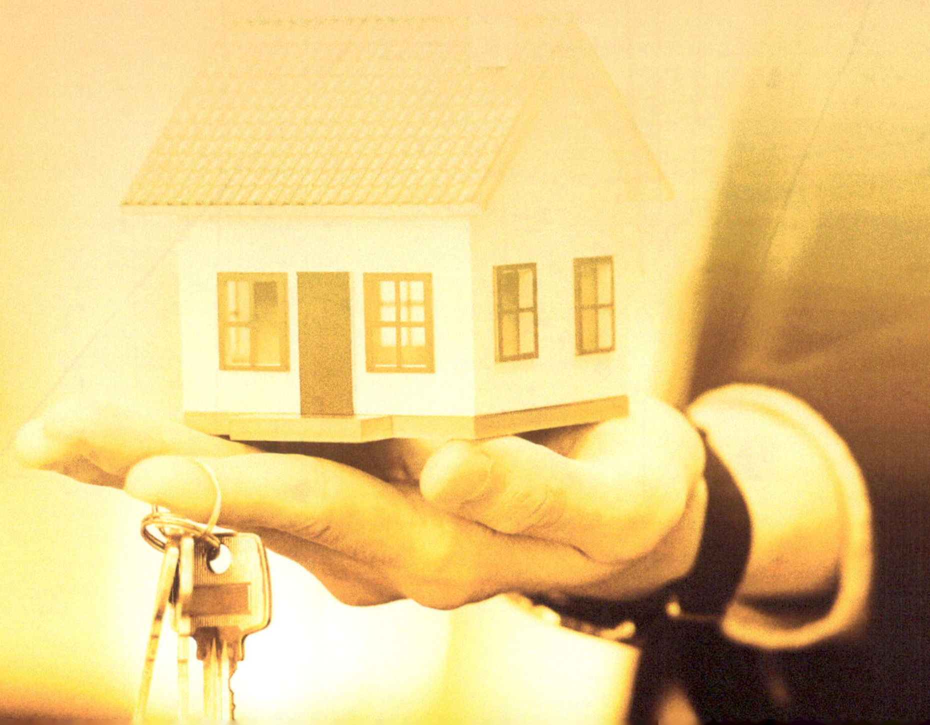

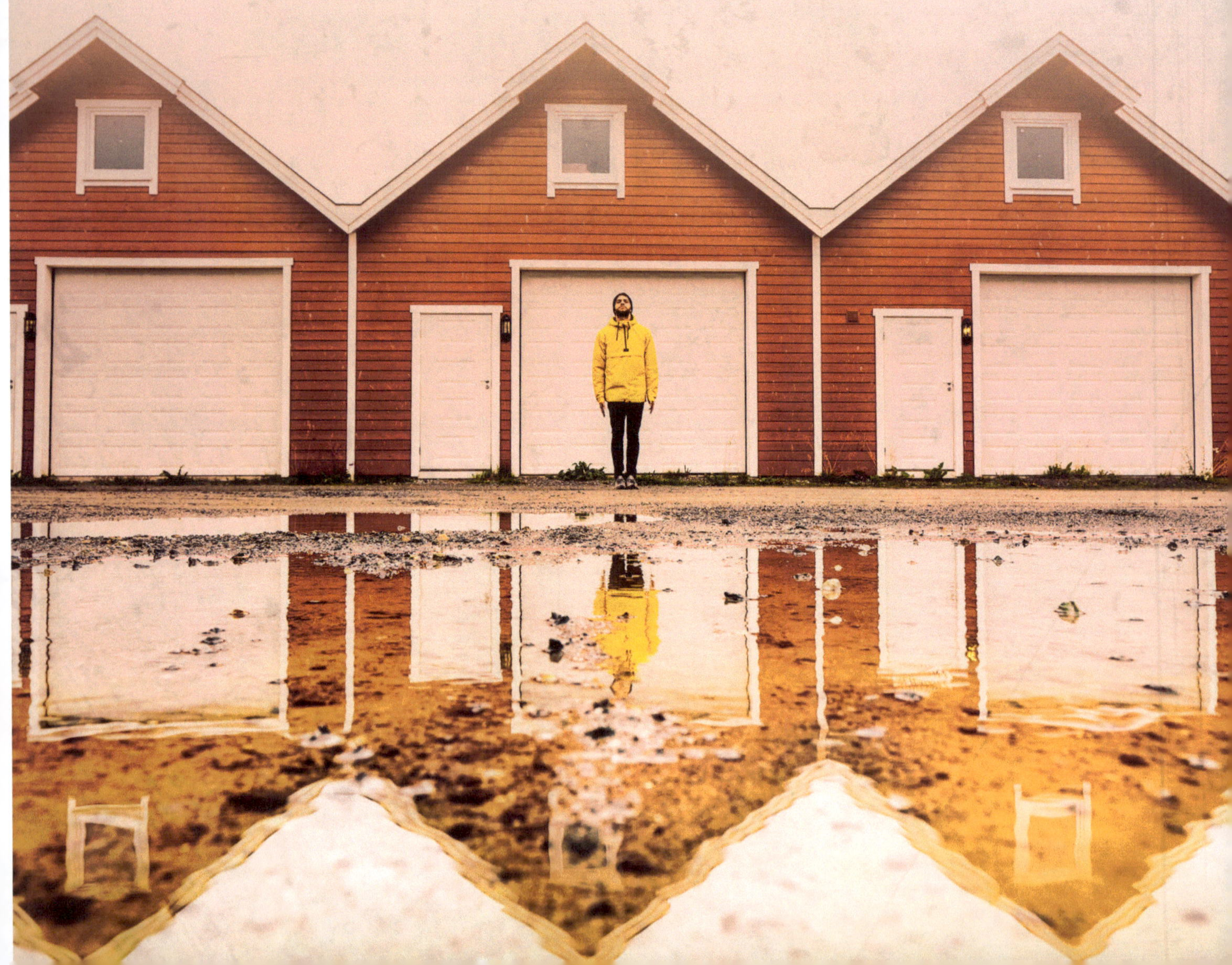
I see the other houses and they seem to have no problems.

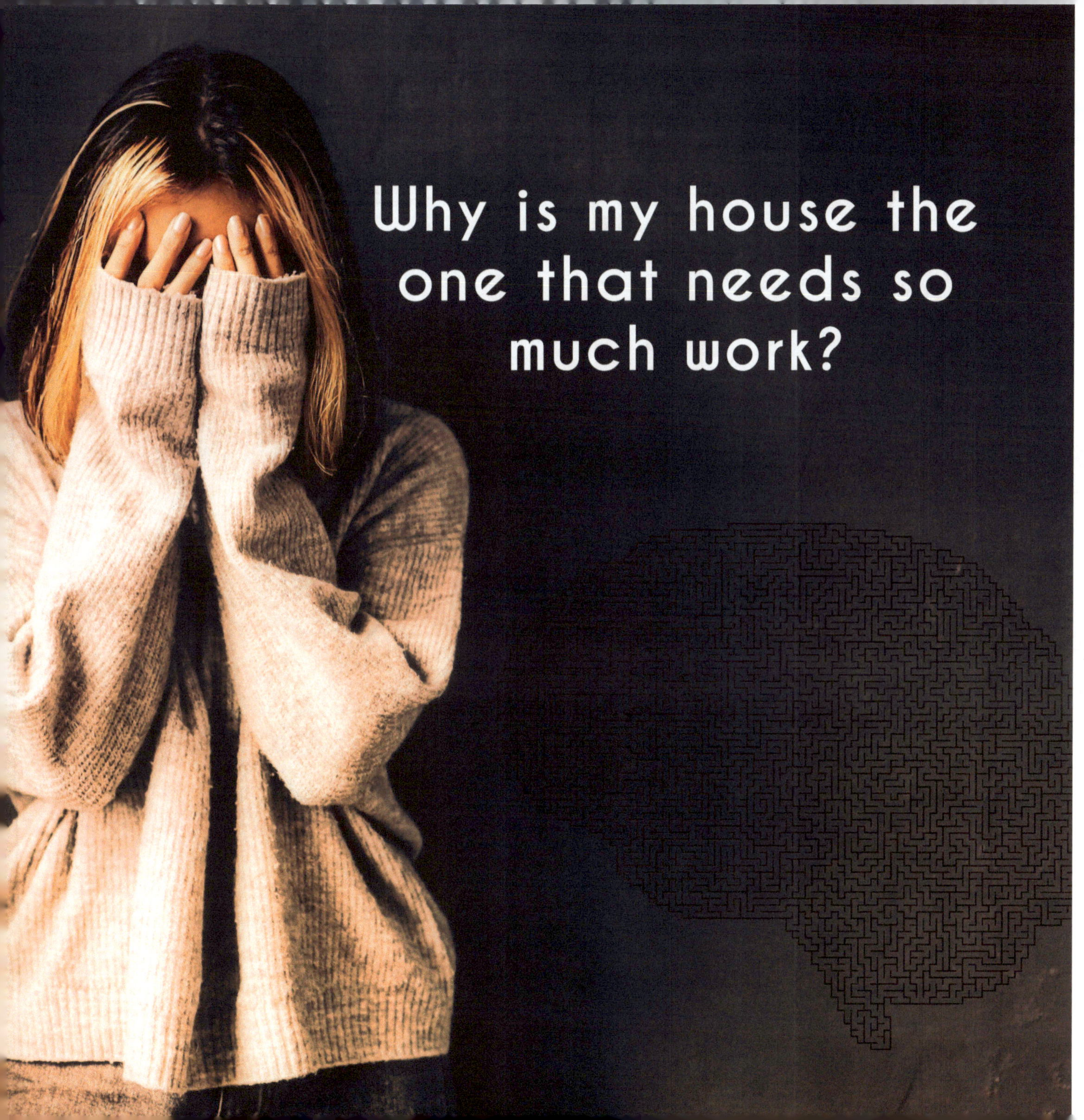
Why is my house the one that needs so much work?

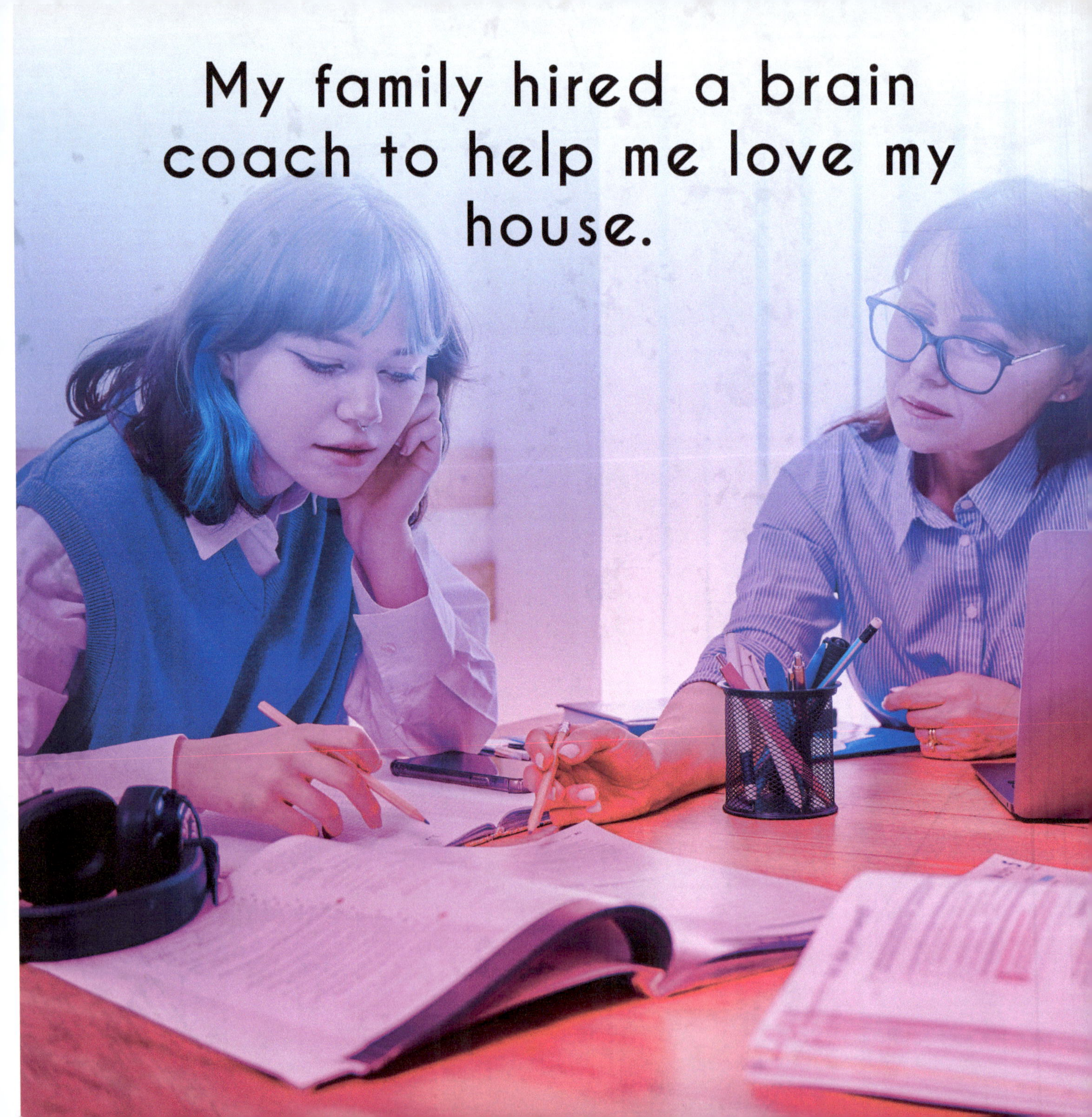
My family hired a brain coach to help me love my house.

She helped me see the beauty
of the colors in my brain.

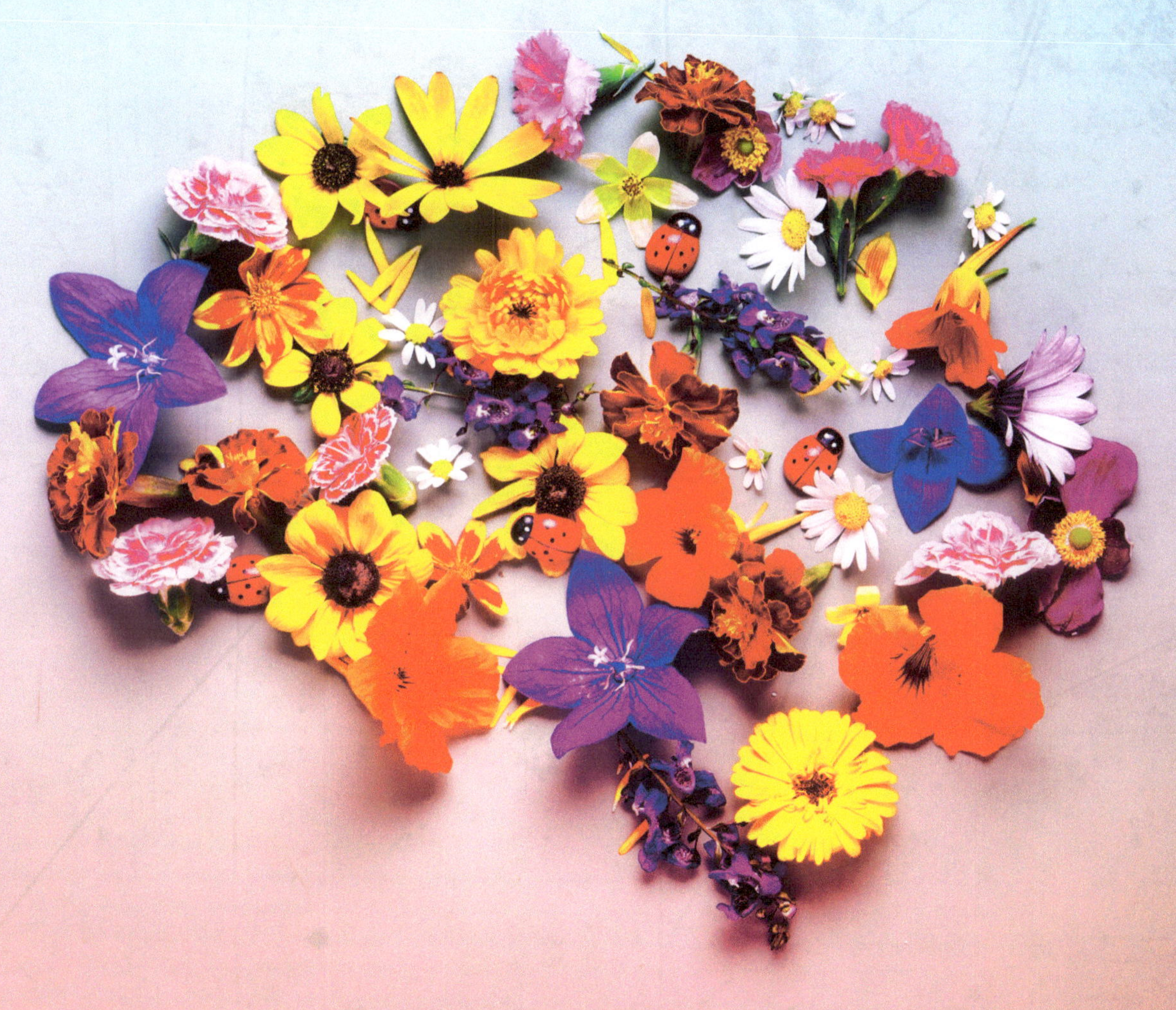

She helped me learn to rewire and polish all the pieces and parts.

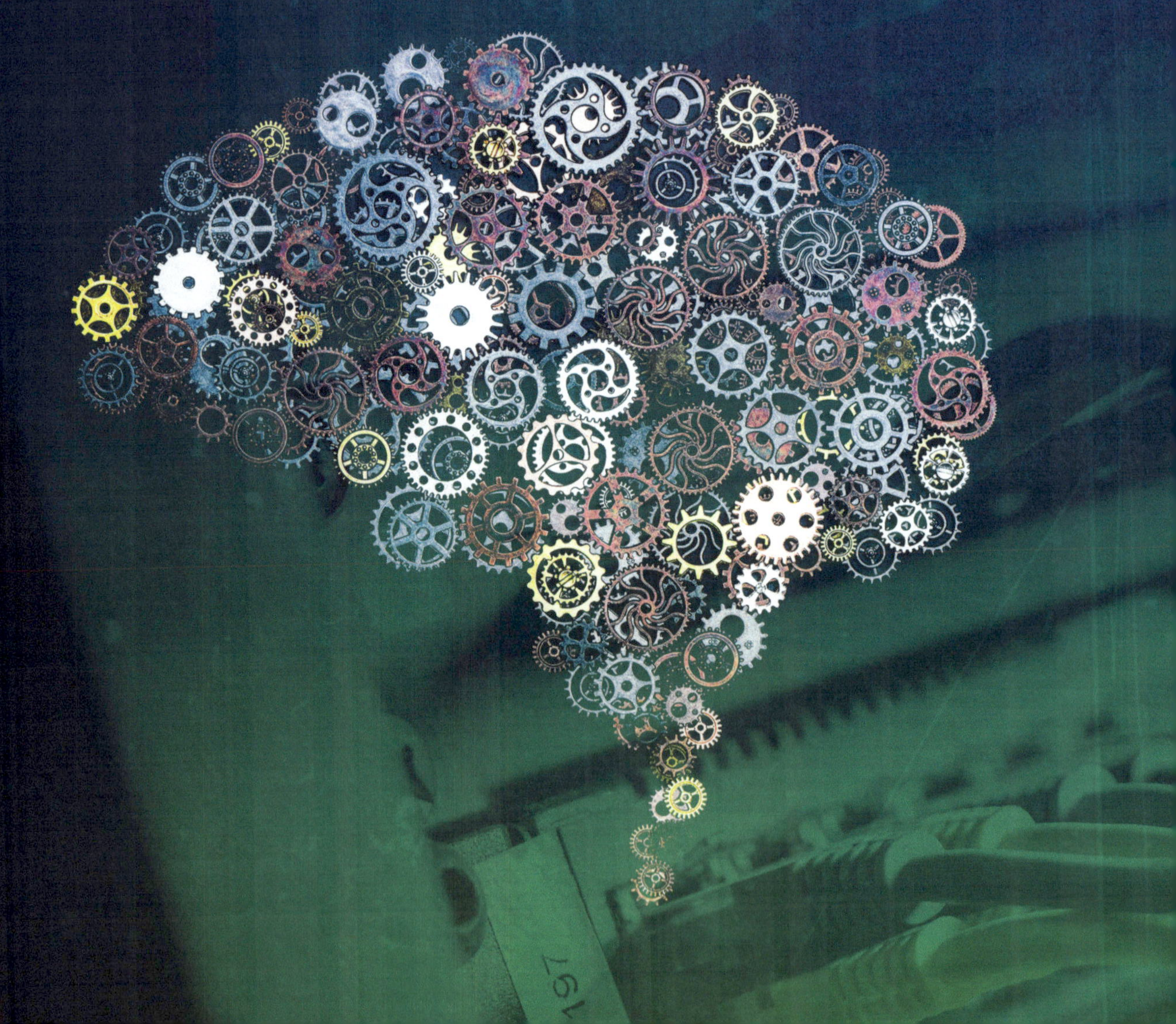

She showed me how to connect the speakers so the volume was in my control.

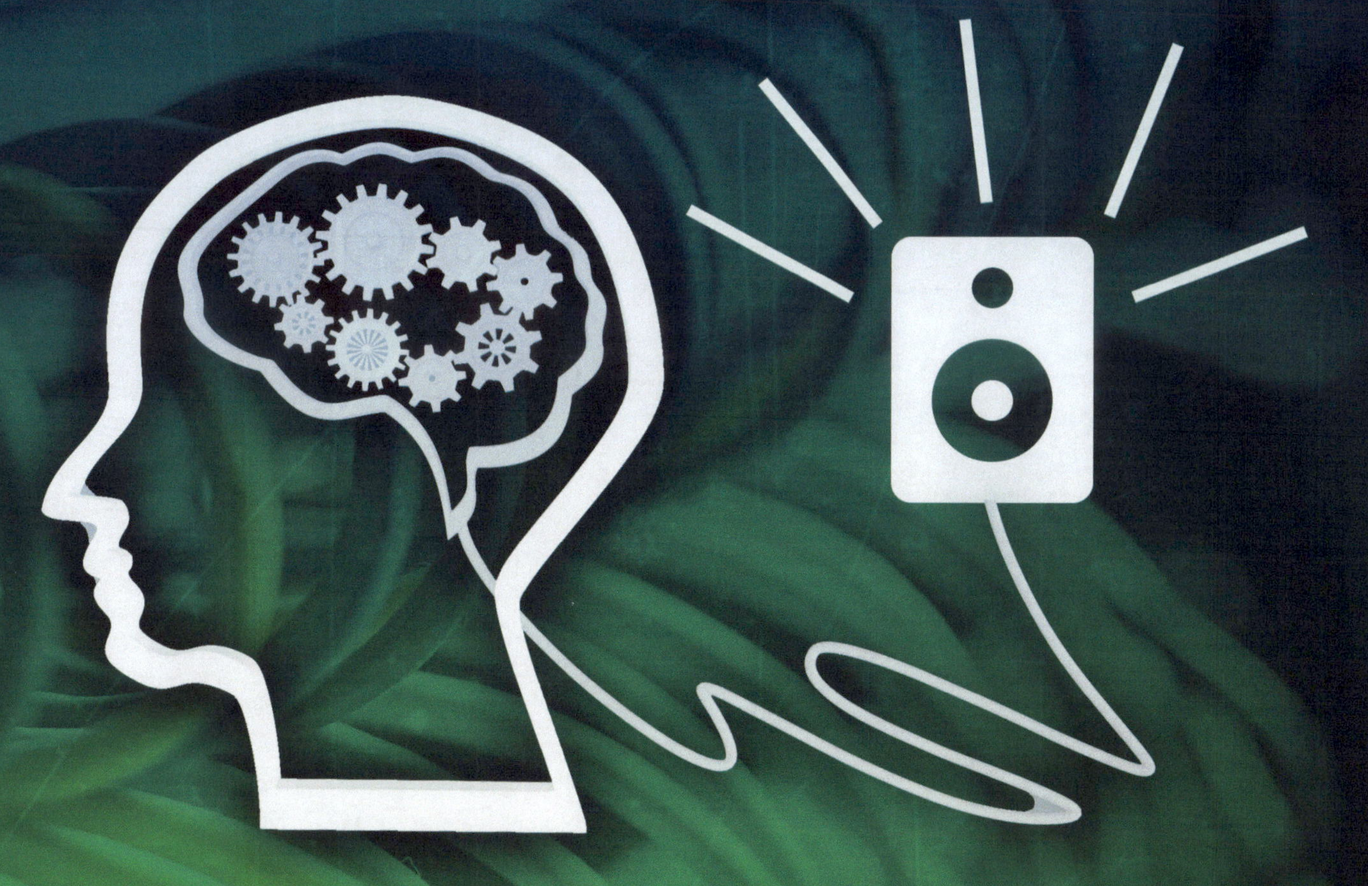

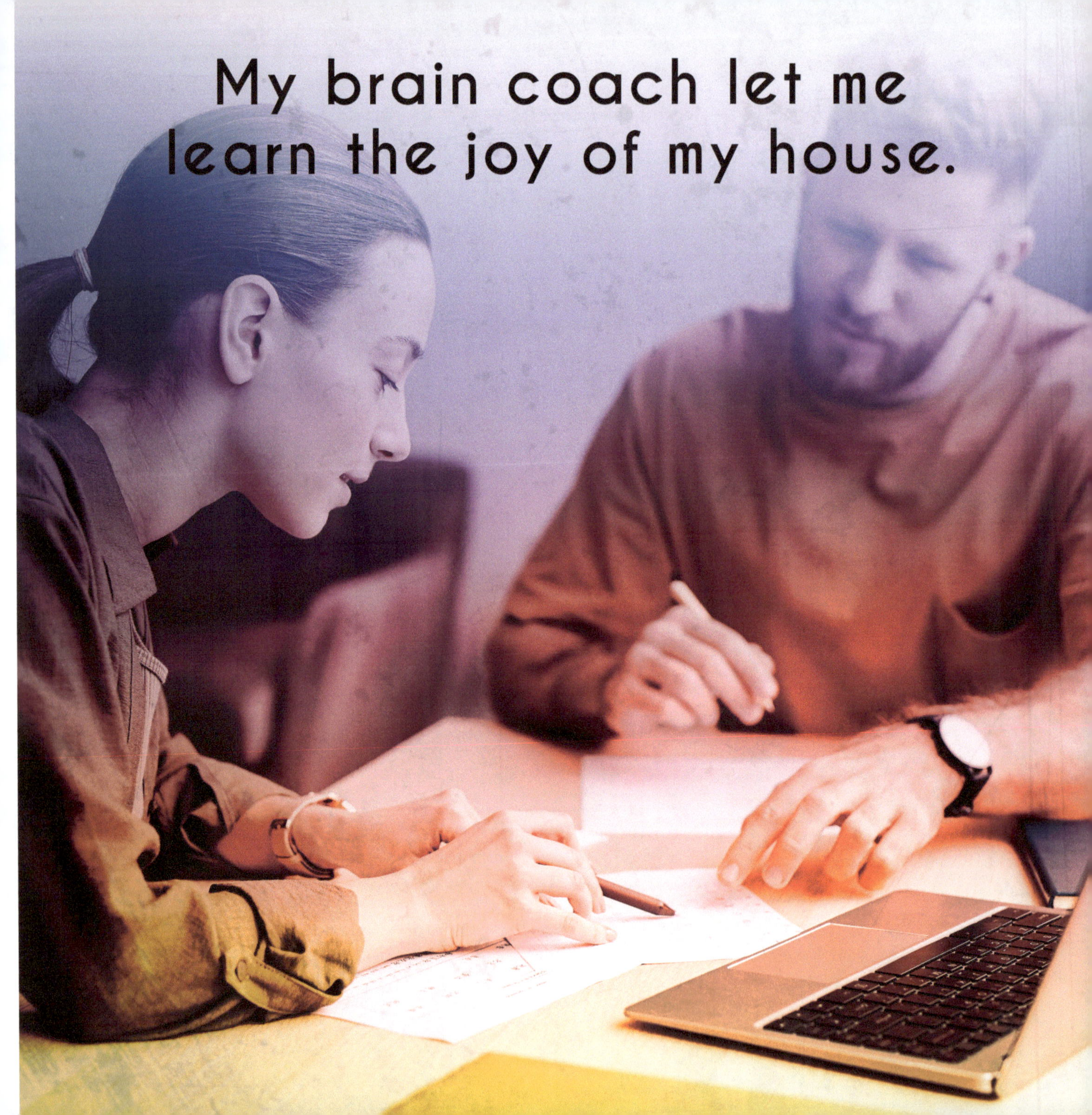
My brain coach let me learn the joy of my house.

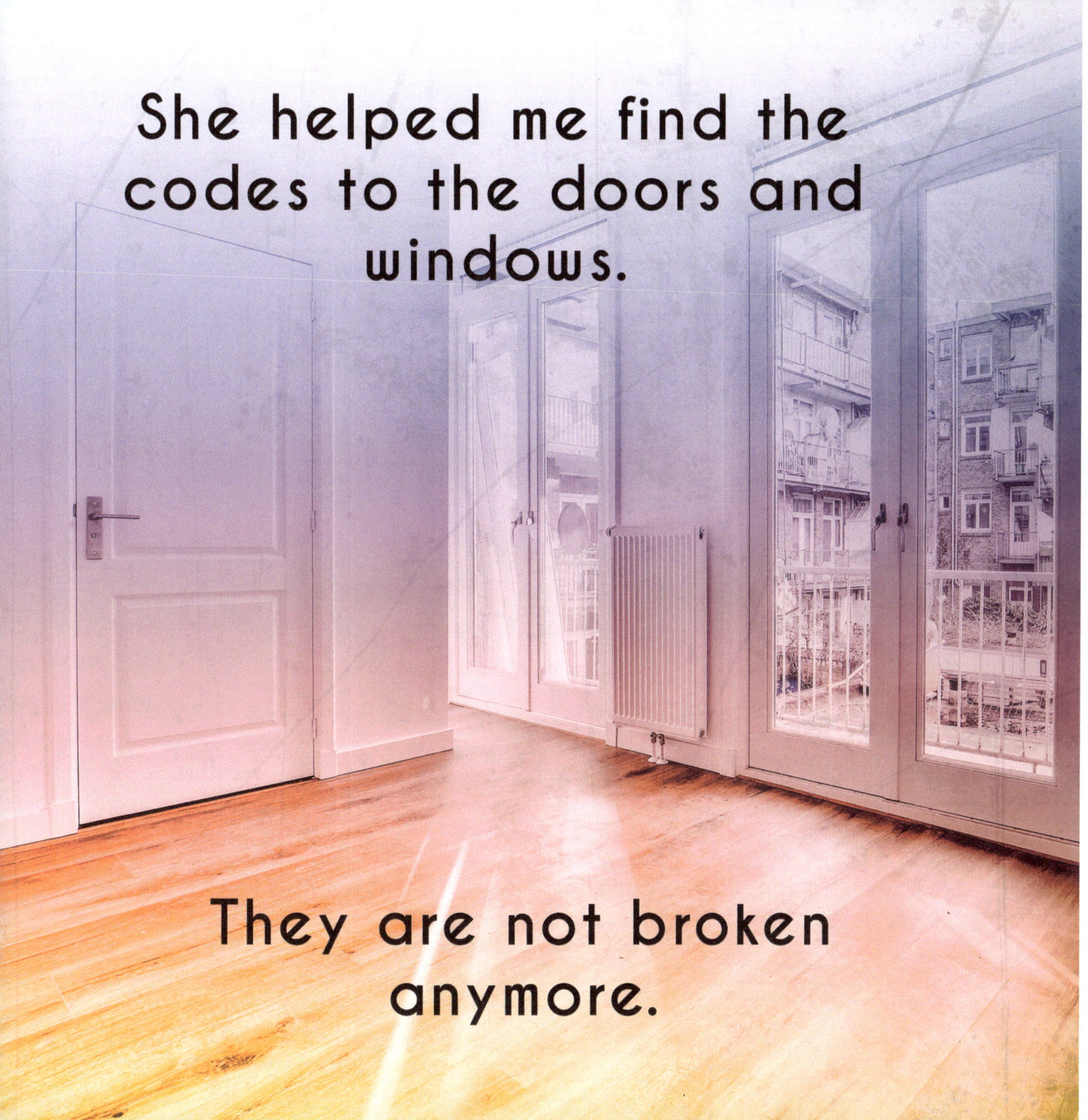
She helped me find the codes to the doors and windows.
They are not broken anymore.

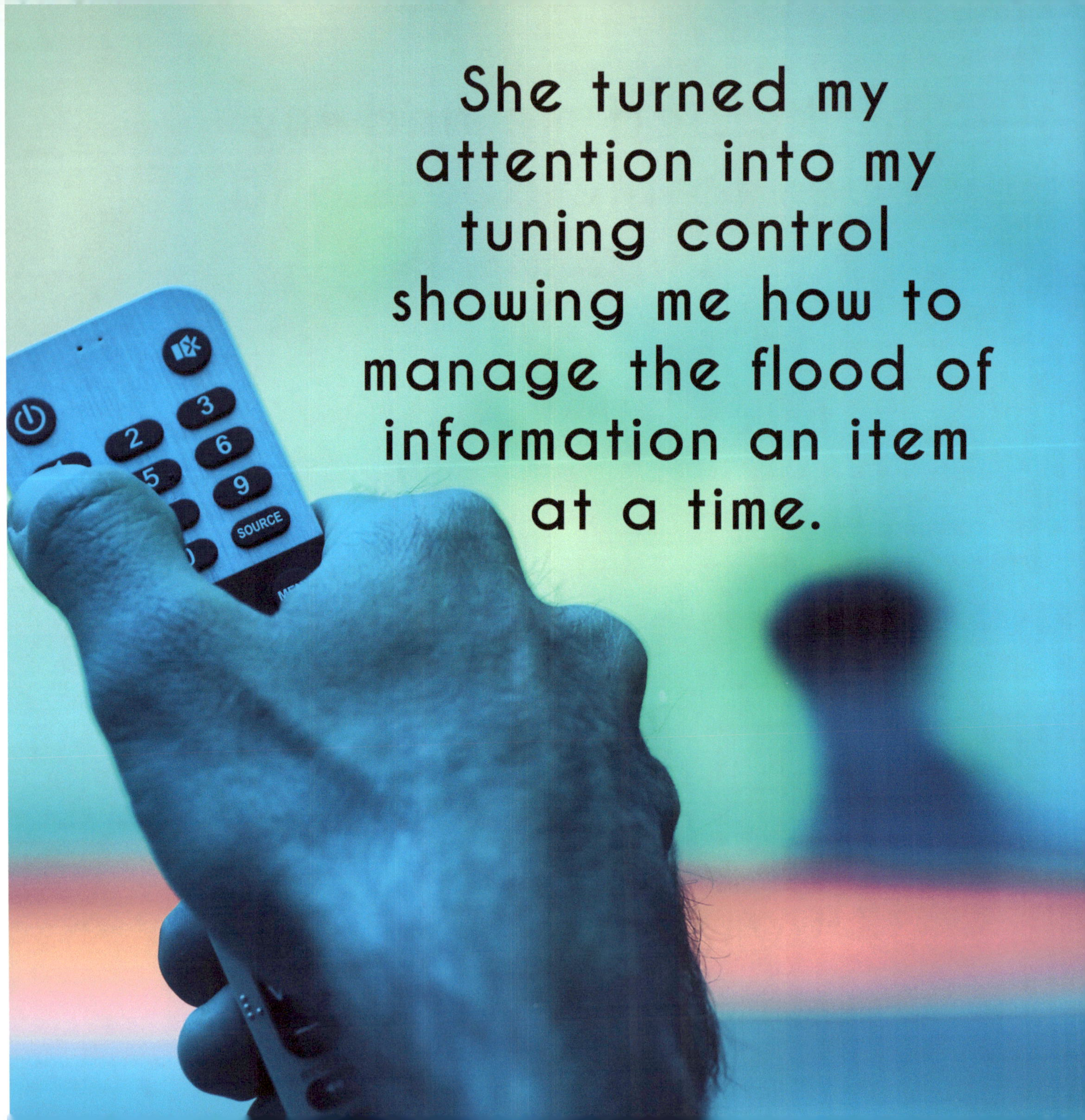

She turned my attention into my tuning control showing me how to manage the flood of information an item at a time.

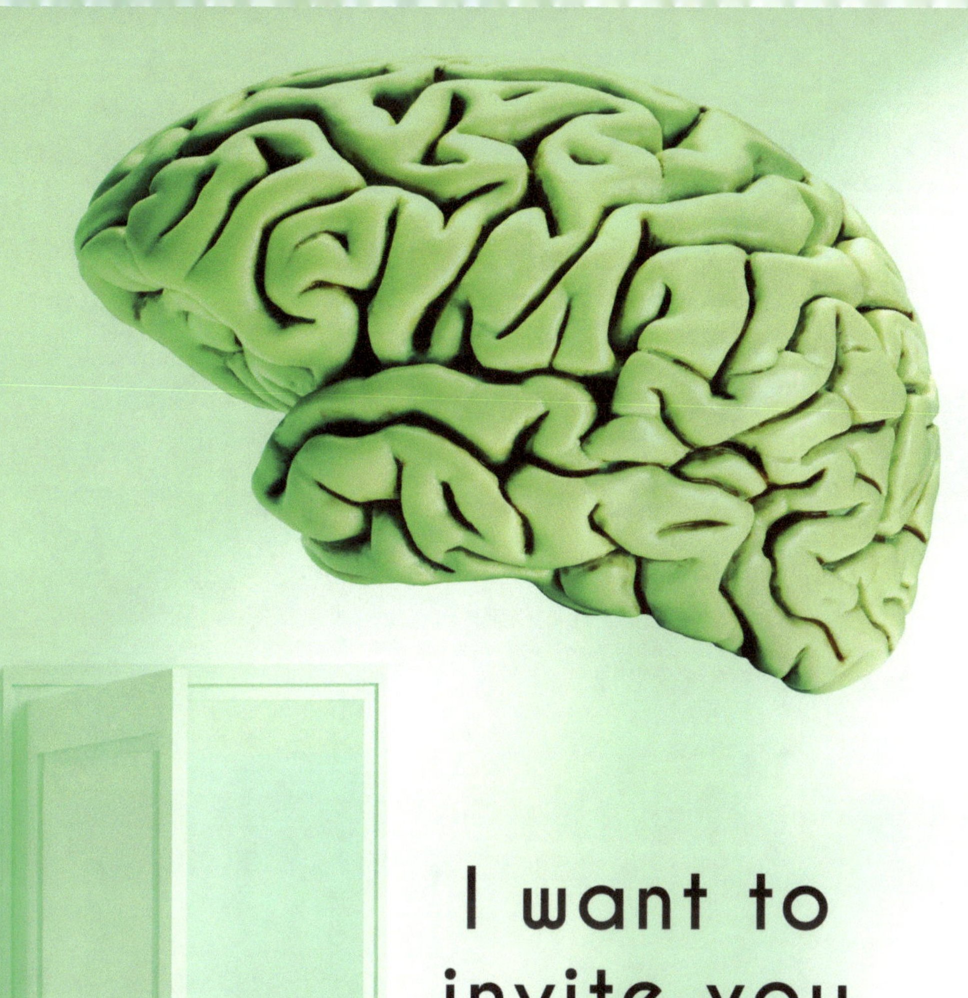

I want to
invite you
to visit my
house now.

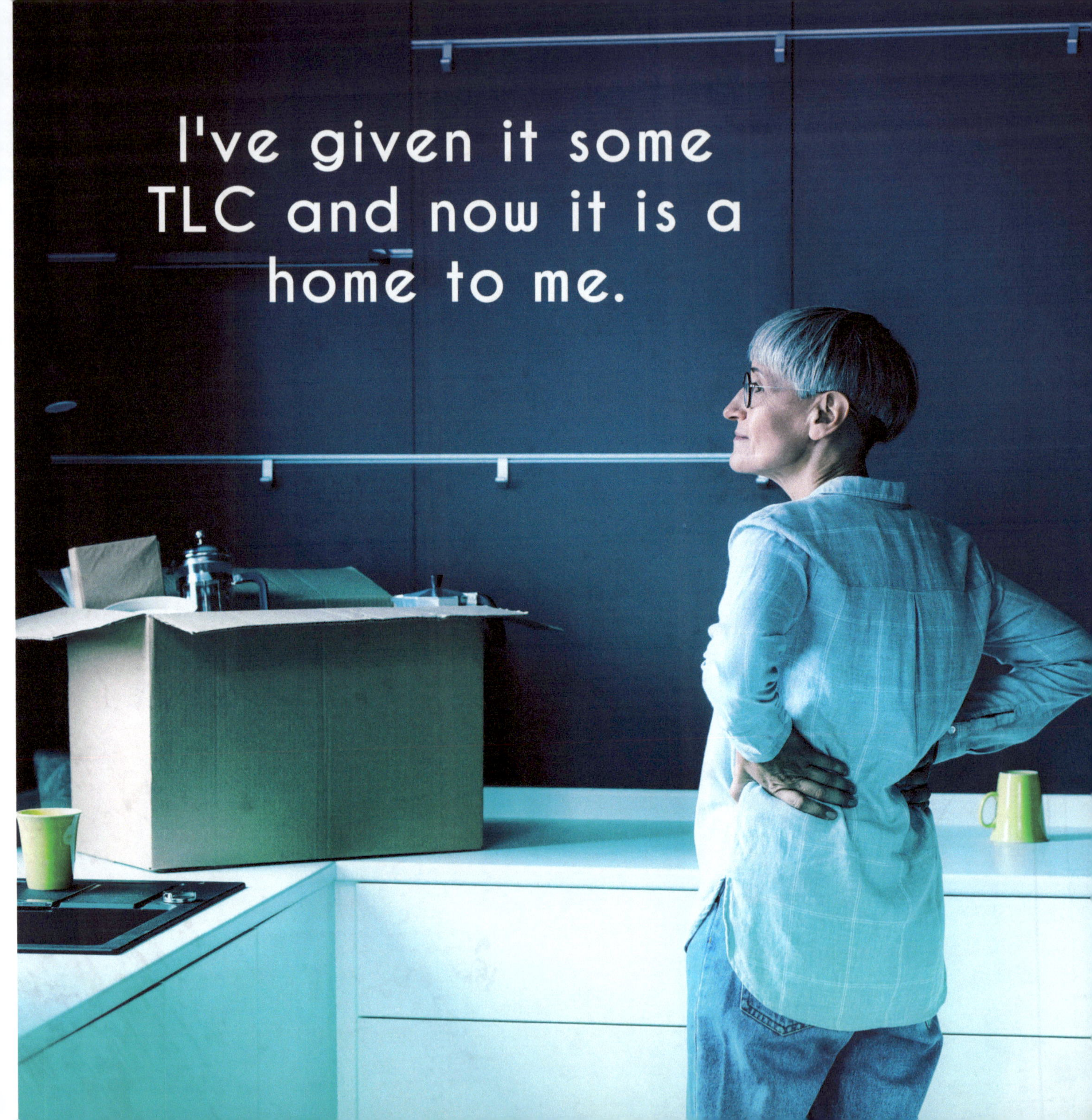
I've given it some TLC and now it is a home to me.

I believe my house is the best there is because I live in it and I am happy and confident in my house.

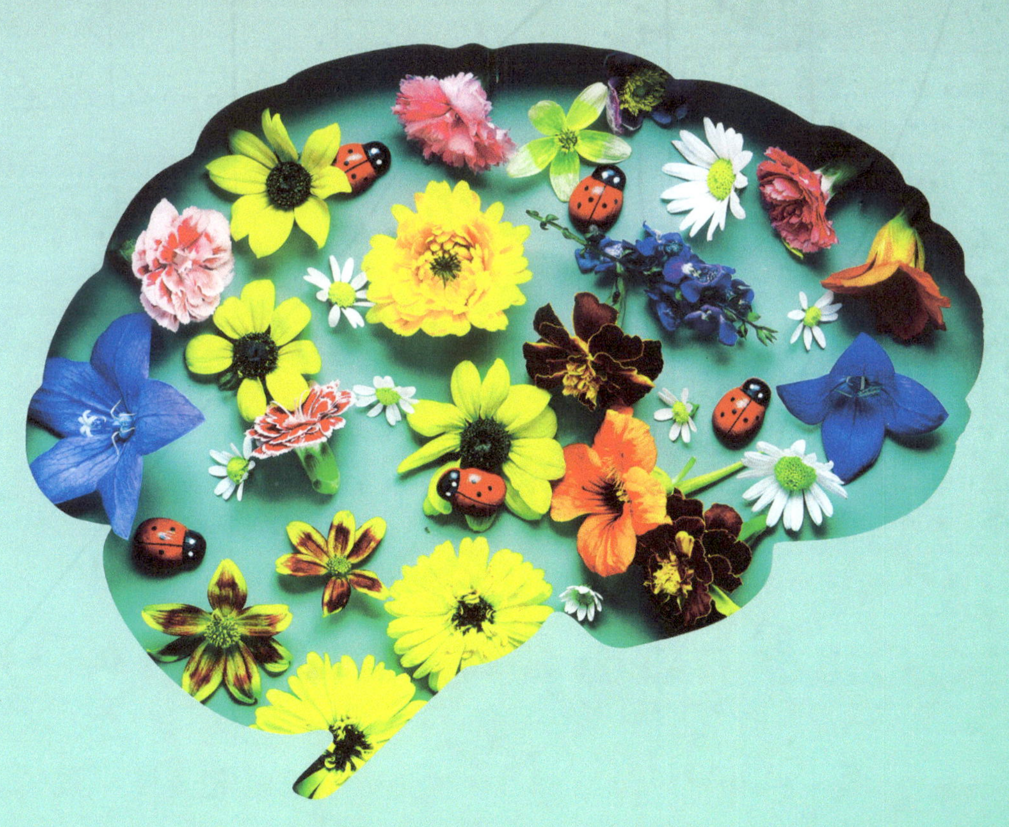

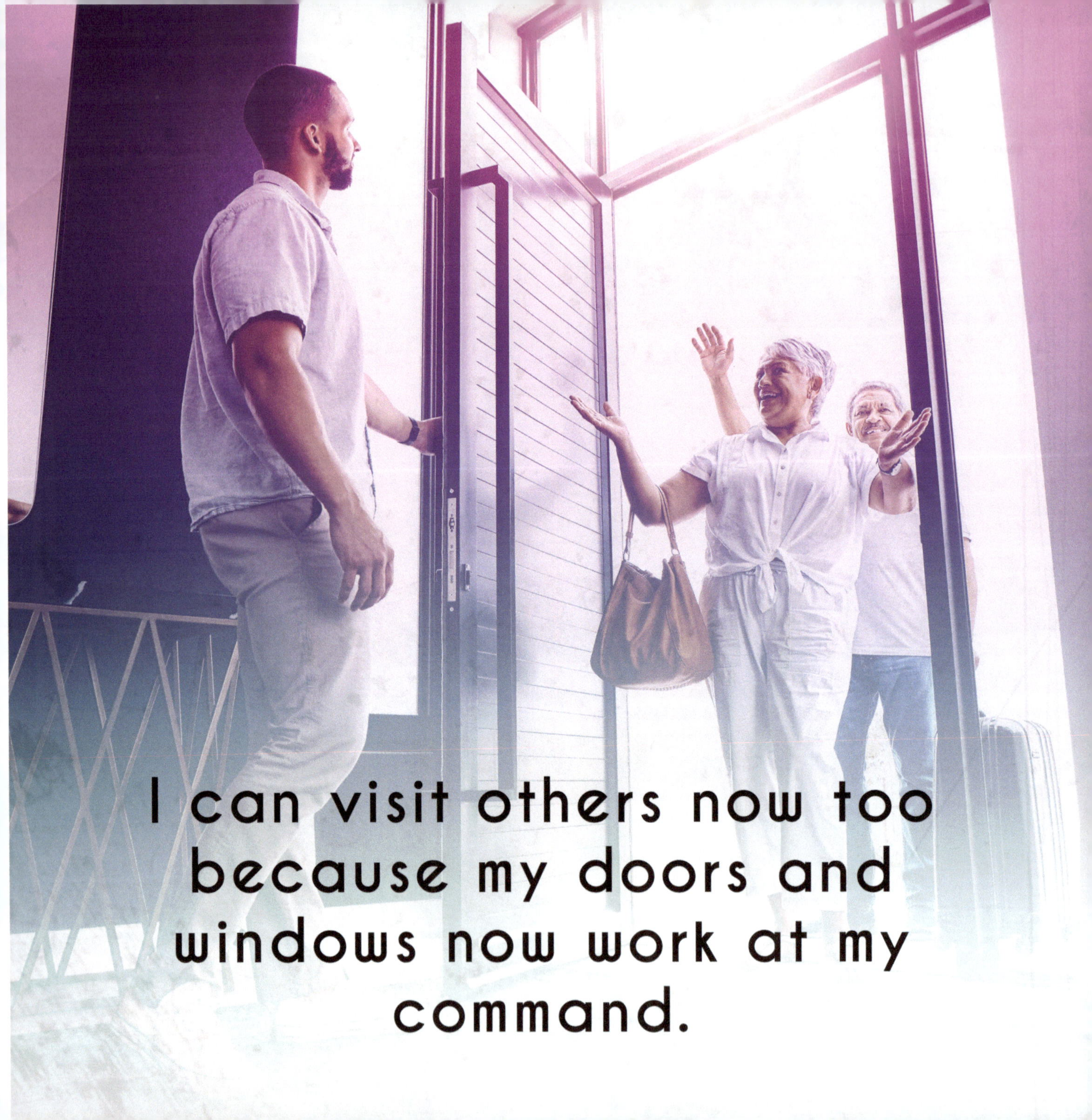

I can visit others now too because my doors and windows now work at my command.

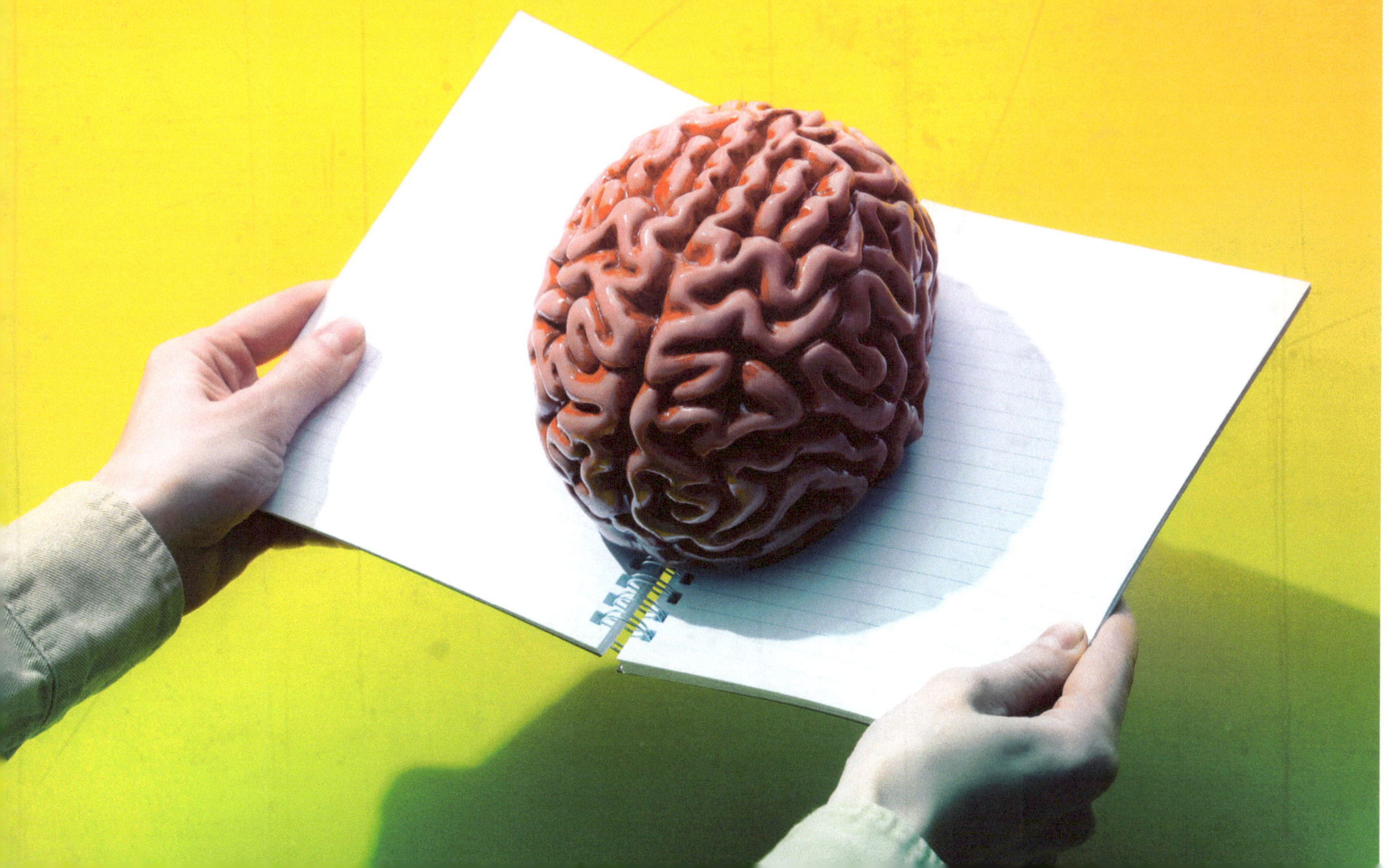

Your house is
uncomfortable you say?
I know how that feels.
Perhaps like me, you need
a little TLC.

A brain trainer can help you to find your way to love your house into your home.

Where to find them? Just ask around or call me up.

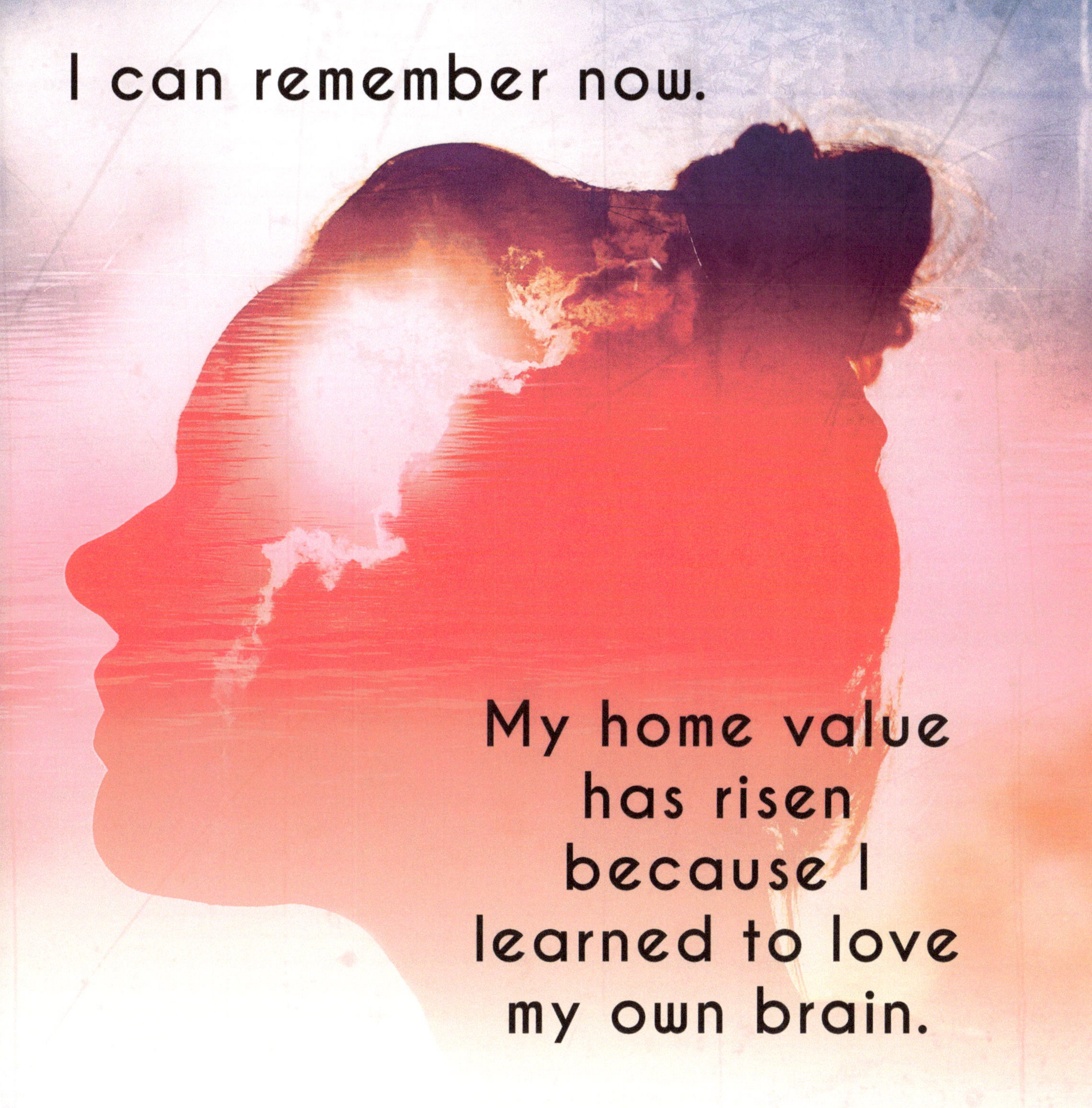
I can remember now.

My home value
has risen
because I
learned to love
my own brain.